The Second Chasm

KAREN V. KIBLER

Wyatt-MacKenzie Publishing, Inc.
DEADWOOD, OREGON

The Second Chasm
by Karen V. Kibler

FIRST EDITION

ISBN: 978-1-932279-31-3

Library of Congress Control Number 2008940954

Wyatt-MacKenzie Publishing, Inc.
DEADWOOD, OREGON

Wyatt-MacKenzie Publishing, Inc., Deadwood, OR
www.WyMacPublishing.com (541) 964-3314

Requests for permission or further information should be addressed to:
Wyatt-MacKenzie Publishing, 15115 Highway 36, Deadwood, Oregon 97430

Dedication

To Ruth,
who inspired the dream
and nurtured it through all its seasons;
and to all those, named and unnamed,
who appear in these pages.

Contents

Foreword

by Joyce Rebeta-Burditt

The Second Chasm, by Karen Kibler, is brave, uncompromising and as compelling as only truth can be. Ms. Kibler takes us on her personal journey through the complicated hell of clinical depression sharing her experience with two major episodes, one triggered by an early divorce and the second by the shocking death of her beloved husband. Through her words we learn the difference between sadness and the kind of clinical depression suffered by so many: the lucky ones diagnosed and in treatment, the unlucky mired in confusion, pain and the sense of unworthiness that makes asking for or receiving help so difficult and which is the most diabolical symptom of this disease. Thanks to Ms. Kibler, we see the face of the monster lurking in the dark and understand its corrosive effects on mind, body and spirit.

If all this sounds like grim going, let me assure you it isn't. Karen's warmth, wit and compassion for her fellow sufferers deliver a message of hope and strength with many smiles along the way. This is not the complaint of a 'victim' written for other 'victims', but rather a guidebook for those of us who have and do struggle with the disease of clinical depression. Karen got better. It's as simple as that. Knowledge made her strong. Determination kept her going. The help she sought provided the answers she needed. As we say in AA, she did the footwork. When she was ready to reach out her hand for help, many hands reached for hers.

According to Karen's account, one of the hands that held her was mine. Quite inadvertently, she picked up a copy of my autobiographical novel *The Cracker Factory*, read it and experienced a "eureka" moment. Reading of my experience with clinical depression which manifested in my case as alcoholism, she discovered that she wasn't alone, wasn't "crazy and was *worthy* of recovery. She states that in a single moment, an absolute stranger changed her life.

So now Karen and I share even more than clinical depression. I also had a eureka moment. Mine came while sitting on a metal stool in a psychiatric ward, defiantly swatting away the helping hands offered to me, rebel to the end as I circled the drain. A moment later, all my defenses crumbled at once, leaving only one insight which I believe was sent by a Higher Power, "I'm in terrible trouble. I can't get well alone."

That was my moment and my beginning. I reached out and could not believe how many hands were ready and willing to lift me up. I could not believe how many absolute strangers gave of their experience, strength and hope to help me get well. Everything these absolute strangers taught me and showed me and helped me to understand went into the writing of *The Cracker Factory*.

My book is their book. Every insight in it was given to me as a gift, by those who knew more than I did at the time. I take no credit. I only passed it on.

Now Karen Kibler has brought her experience, strength and hope full circle and is passing it on for the only reason that counts: she hopes it will help other people. She has bravely gone back into her past to relive the most painful times in her life in order to place them squarely in the context of her recovery. What she's telling us is that recovery is possible. Happiness is possible. She lays out some guideposts for us to follow. She asks us to consider the effect on our family and friends if we don't ask for help, an important question seldom asked. She takes us by the hand and leads us on her own twisting trail to recovery pointing out both the traps and the triumphs, helping us to better see both in our own lives.

We find ourselves, when at the end of our journey with Karen, admiring her hard-won strength, heartened by her message and grateful that she invited us along.

Karen got better. So did I. So will you. Reach out. Help is waiting.

Prologue

I'm not sure where we were exactly when it happened. We were driving from Washington D.C. to Arizona, by a route that included Knoxville, Tennessee and Austin, Texas. My sister had been working in D.C., and was moving back to her permanent home in Arizona. I was along to keep her company on the trip. What I do remember exactly is the feeling of being released, of cutting the tether to a dark and hidden place within me that had been carefully camouflaged to prevent any eye from penetrating the mask that hid my secret, a secret about a time many years before, when I had thought I must be insane. In the space of a moment, a total stranger was able to shatter the self-imposed chain that had held me captive for years. The stranger's name is Joyce Rebeta-Burditt, and I was reading her book, *The Cracker Factory*.

Ruth hated it that I could read while traveling in a car. When it was my turn to drive, she couldn't read because it quickly made her carsick. However, I had no such problem, and I liked to pass the hours by reading while she drove. This was a source of great irritation to her, so I compromised: while I was reading, she was free to start conversations at any time, and I would respond to her. Often, I read the same sentence five to ten times before comprehending its meaning, as I juggled the fulfillment of my agreement and the pleasure of reading. Frequently, though, Ruth was absorbed in her own thoughts, which allowed me the chance to continue reading the author's tale.

The Cracker Factory was a popular book at the time, though I don't remember what had prompted me to choose it for the drive. Normally, I read adventure novels – murder mysteries, spy capers, medical thrillers. The fact that I chose that book, a novel about a woman alcoholic who experiences clinical depression, rather than one more typical of my interests, was one of the little miracles that happens to each of us in such unnoticed and unheralded whispers. It was the author's simple description of one character's inability to enter a grocery store that changed my world when I read the words.

Still today, I can feel the slight hesitation as my mind attempted to access a place I had kept walled off all those years. My pulse quickened as my heart gradually recognized that this secret place I had valiantly succeeded in hiding from everyone, *was not inhabited by me alone.* This was an astonishing discovery, and the joy in my soul bubbled into laughter and tears of relief and gratitude. I wasn't alone, and I wasn't crazy! And this was wonderful!

That day in the car, in July of 1982, was to become the midpoint of my story of depression and survival. My life prior to that day is one arm of the story, and my life from that day onward is the other arm; my discovery in the car that day was the pivotal moment between the two.

CHAPTER 1
Young Love

1970		1976		July, 1982		1987		Now
Chapter 1								

It's really one of the great perils of life that teenagers of every generation are convinced that no one knows life's truths quite as well as they do. If anything in this life has led me to the brink of questioning the divine wisdom in which I truly do believe, it is the baffling subspecies we call *teens*. As a teenager, I was no exception.

My childhood was filled with love and nurturing. I always felt safe, I had reasonable rules, and I had no concept of limitations on my aspirations. My future was there for the seizing, and I knew I could follow whichever star beckoned me. So of course I set my sights on marrying my high school sweetheart during the Christmas break following high school graduation. My reasoning was lofty and sophisticated, the most mature thought process imaginable: this was during the years of the Vietnam draft lottery, and with my boyfriend drawing the number thirty-five, I concluded that I would prefer to be a widow than to be a broken-hearted fiancée. Really, that was my logic.

Of course, it is obvious to me today that I had absolutely no foundation for such a conclusion; I certainly had no knowledge of what it meant to lose a husband or a fiancé for any reason, let alone because he had died. My attitude was naïve at best, and remarkably insensitive toward those who had actually experienced widowhood. Yet I can remember thinking (and possibly stating with a little drama) those exact words. We were in love, and surely nothing else mattered. When our families first suggested to us, and then pleaded with us to think again ... to perhaps wait a few years ... we were certain they "**just didn't understand**."

How many times have you heard a similar impassioned statement from someone under the age of, well, the age of sanity? Undaunted by any voice, of reason or otherwise, we ventured into marital bliss and started to build a life together. Ironically, the spring after our wedding, Terry was able to enlist in the Air National Guard, and so he never even participated in the draft.

We really were happy; our love was real and we shared a vision of our future. Our first year wasn't an easy one, but it was a loving one.

Terry and I had known each other since junior high, but didn't begin to date until near the end of my junior, and Terry's senior, year of high school. We attended the same church, where I often accompanied him when he sang for services. At school we were in many of the same musical groups. The week before my high school graduation, Terry asked my parents if it would be all right with them if he gave me a diamond ring for graduation. He was asking for my hand in marriage! For the next few months, we thought it would be years before we actually had a wedding; then came the draft lottery, and our resulting change in plans. We would have the wedding in December, and until then, would each continue to live at home.

In the fall we commuted the 20 miles or so from our town (population 1,800) to the community college in the "city" (population 31,000). That summer after my graduation, and into our first semester in the fall, we earned extra money by clearing a grove of dead trees. In the Midwest, every farm has a grove of trees, to act as a wind and snow break. Some friends of ours didn't have time to do the clearing on their own and hired us to do the job. It occurred to me later that perhaps they just pretended to be too busy, because they were generous enough of heart that they could have made it up just to provide us a way to earn a little extra money.

Armed with a chainsaw, we worked for a few hours each day before or after our regular jobs, and on Saturdays, to cut down the plentiful saplings and small trees that had sprouted between the big trees. Some of the trees were too big for us to handle on our own, and our friends helped us with those; we used a tractor and chain to safely control the direction the trees fell. But for the ones we could handle, Terry cut the notch as I pushed on the tree, and after it fell we cut it into smaller branches and stacked it to dry for firewood. We worked well together, and getting dirty and sweaty working outdoors was a nice change of pace from the restaurant where I waited tables and the grocery store where Terry clerked.

We did have one mishap that has remained one of my most touching memories to this day. If you have ever used a chainsaw, you are familiar with how it "jumps" sometimes as it comes in contact with the wood. When the arm jumps, the blade doesn't care what happens to be in its way – even if it is someone's leg. The accident occurred when I was standing a bit too close to the tree as Terry began his cut – the blade jumped and dug right into my kneecap instead of the tree.

As you might imagine, being cut by a chainsaw is unpleasant. Had it contacted the fleshy part of my calf or thigh, I'm sure the result would have been different. By biting into my kneecap, it hit my skeletal structure, and set off vibrations the entire length of my leg. I imagine that this is what it would feel like if you stood on top of a jackhammer as it hammered. Not that I've done that of course, but it's challenging to find a good analogy for a chainsaw buzz. Convinced that my leg had been amputated and was hanging only by a few threads of my skin and my blue jeans, I screamed in horror. Although my memory of the ensuing sequence of events is a little hazy at this point because what I remember most is the terror and hysteria I was feeling, I think that Terry slapped me. Just like in the Abbott and Costello movies, I think he slapped me. He had to get my attention some way, and there wasn't a 2x4 handy. He needed to tell me that my leg was intact – a little bloody, but certainly **not** virtually amputated.

He carried me to the house so that we could get a

closer look at the damage. He was gentle and loving as he helped me clean and bandage the wound. Following a tetanus shot and a few weeks to heal, I was left with nothing more permanent than a jagged scar and a great story to tell.

This turned out to be only the first time Terry carried me after an injury; in hindsight, maybe the incident should have been a sign to him to think twice about this marriage. Had he done so, he might have been able to see that our marriage would involve a lot of "carrying" one another, that it would require a willingness to put the needs of someone else first until firm footing could be regained, and a commitment to find healing together as he had felt that day in the grove.

The second accident occurred when we had only been married eight months. I totaled our car in an accident. It was our only car, so Terry was home without transportation when the fireman called to tell him his wife had been taken to the hospital after an accident. The fireman hung up before explaining that I had no life-threatening injuries, so Terry called a friend who had to drive forty-five minutes to get him. Rather than sitting at home waiting for the friend to arrive, Terry started walking to the hospital, a good fifteen miles away. That was not a silly teenager walking along the highway; that was my husband, who had no idea whether or not I was going to survive until he got there.

Luckily, his friend found him along the highway, and drove him the rest of the way. Following my release from the hospital, we had to wait a time before my appointment with the doctor who would see what could be done about my very broken nose – I had broken the steering wheel with my nose! Terry and his friend were hungry, so we stopped at a fast food place for lunch. While waiting to place the order, I experienced a sudden wave of severe nausea and needed to find the restroom quickly.

Terry got the attention of an employee, who came outside with us to unlock the restroom door. Remember, this was in the early 70s, when fast food restaurants had locked restrooms that were located outside. As Terry walked with the employee, he turned to look at me just in time to see me falling to the sidewalk as I fainted. Rushing back to me, he scooped me into his arms before I hit the concrete, carrying me for a second time.

When I awoke in the car, I noticed that he was all wet, and asked how he got that way. "As you fainted, you sort of 'wet' me," he said with a smile. But even this was not his last assaulting event of the day. You can just imagine what all the other occupants of the doctor's waiting room were thinking as we walked through the door: with my hair all awry, my nose bent and bloody, my eyes already turning black and blue, my dress torn – Terry knew they all thought that my damage was husband-inflicted. This loving young man who had just walked miles rather than waiting at home for his ride to arrive, and who had gallantly saved me from yet further potential injury in a nasty fall only to be rewarded by a dousing with urine, was now being given the evil eye from those who thought they knew the source of my battering.

Three months later, while Terry was in active duty in the Air National Guard, and I was at a Laundromat between classes at the university, our mobile home caught fire during some warranty repairs. I came home to see windows of black gaping spaces where there should have been curtains. We lost nearly everything in the fire, and our Irish setter had been badly burned. The Red Cross loaned Terry the money to fly home, and we spent the next few days trying to salvage what we could.

It had been a tough year, but we were still smiling – after all, we had a new car and a new mobile home with clean carpeting!

CHAPTER 2
Sustainability

1970		1976		July, 1982		1987		Now
	Chapter 2							

Married life suited me well. I was finally an adult and was an equal with my siblings. All my life, I had been the outsider in the family. The span of years separating my four older siblings is five years and eight months. The span separating the youngest of those four and myself is five years and six months.

The oldest four had many experiences in common: two of my sisters dated the same guy (at the same time, no less!); they all four went on family vacations together; they performed in the school band together; had leading roles in plays together; were on athletic teams at the same time; went to the same parties and had the same friends; and all had stories of life on the farm. All four had been successful in school – more than just getting good grades, they were popular, athletic, and talented. They were a tough act to follow!

When I was in elementary school, I was just a little kid who listened to their parties when I was supposed to be asleep, stayed home when they went on dates, and bragged about them to my friends as I watched their games, attended the plays, and heard the concerts. By the time I got to high school, they were all married, had been or were currently attending college, and had nothing in common with me. Unlike the four of them, I didn't make the debate team or the basketball team, and I never had a leading role.

But marriage brought me into their ranks at last! I wasn't as different from them as I had been in the past. Now we had something in common, and that was very important to me.

Terry and I believed that we would live happily ever after, that nothing could ever put our relationship at risk. Divorce was far less common then, and for the most part, our friends believed along with us that marriage was forever. At that time, I had not yet met anyone who could consider that if a marriage didn't work out, one could always leave it and start with someone new. Years later, I did hear that attitude voiced occasionally. We certainly knew of people, sometimes good friends or family members, who had been divorced, but it was still uncommon and something no one believed could happen to them. So we believed that vows spoken were vows kept, and surely love could conquer all. Maybe that's true for some, but for others the love just starts to lose its strength and as it disintegrates, it ceases to be.

A year and a half into our marriage, we moved to Iowa City, where Terry went back to college to get a degree in business. I quit college and went to work full time. I didn't mind the change in pace for me, and we were both supportive of the other's career goals. Terry's new Bachelor's Degree program did not give him credit for the courses he had taken to earn his Associate Degree, so we knew he had four to five years of college ahead of him. Because he continued to work part time jobs, he took just enough credit hours to qualify as a full time student.

The school year started, we met new friends, we had a great life, and we thought about starting a family; however, something changed for us that year. As the school year progressed, Terry's life became more focused on university interactions and functions that didn't include me; we spent less time together. By spring, our relationship was faltering. Maybe we had tried to grow up too quickly, and left too much childhood unlived. Maybe as our roles changed, there were just so many distractions and diversions that a clear path for us as a couple was no longer visible. We talked about splitting up and going our separate ways, about always remaining the best of friends no matter what. In our immaturity, it was almost an adventure to contemplate an act so bold as to separate. We even sought guidance from a marriage counselor at the university. Each of us became critical of the other, and we used the counseling sessions as a way to express unkind accusations. As we continued to drift apart emotionally, we made plans for Terry to move out as soon as we could manage it financially.

Then Terry left for two weeks of Air National Guard duty, and I received the untimely news that I was pregnant. For ten days I told no one, and I thought of little else but what might be waiting in my – in our – future. This life just starting to make its way into the world could not be my husband's quicksand; I could embrace the marriage – or maybe even the end of the marriage – but not a marriage of entrapment or commitment by guilt from a husband who yearned to leave. So when Terry returned from Guard camp, I first asked if he had thought about us and what we should do with our   marriage. His answer was that he thought we would be fine, and that we could make it work. "That's good," I replied, "because we're having a baby."

Our pregnancy was one of the happiest times of my life. We laughed, we planned, we rediscovered our relationship. Our son was born on Christmas Day, 1973. All the other patients had been allowed to go home on Christmas Eve, so we had the undivided attention of the hospital staff. The nurses dressed Shane in a little red elf suit, and Terry – who had been awake all night with me – went home to have hot dogs for Christmas dinner. It seemed that the world was ours again.

At age seven days, Shane was the youngest attendee at our friends' New Year's Eve party a week later. We celebrated with our friends while Shane slept upstairs. Terry was so proud, and so attentive to our new baby.

Shane grew up with our cat and our new Irish setter puppy. I was so lucky to be able to stay home with him for his first eight months. Shane did, and still does today, look just like his dad, and he was an exceptionally good baby in the sense that he slept a lot. It's much easier to be a new mom when the baby of the house sleeps all night and most of the day. When Shane was only five months old we took a long road trip to Arizona. We drove straight through, but it still took maybe thirty-six hours or so. Shane slept and played and looked out the window, and only near the end of the trip did we hear him cry.

In the fall, I went back to school, so both Shane's parents were college students again. Raising a small child while attending college is a stressful undertaking, and it is quite a responsibility. I had changed my major, and found that my new courses were more difficult than I had anticipated. Terry didn't get to spend much time with us between his course load and his part time job. For a year or so we struggled but managed to keep moving forward.

The next school year, the fall of 1975, we experienced another change in distribution of responsibility: I was the one to work part time along with classes, and Terry devoted more time to school. He joined a business fraternity, and spent most of his free time involved in the fraternity activities. Shane and I spent most of our evenings without Terry, and we both missed him.

In December of that year we celebrated Christmas and our fifth anniversary out of town with Terry's parents, and then came back to our home in Iowa City just in time for New Year's Eve. We tried to get a babysitter so that we could attend the New Year's Eve party being held by Terry's business fraternity, but when we couldn't reach anyone, I told him to go without me. Later that evening, a friend for whom we had left a message earlier phoned; he was happy to baby-sit, so I called Terry and told him

I would be at the party soon. As I mingled with his frater- nity brothers, the remark I heard again and again after being introduced to them was, "I didn't know Terry was married." That night should have been a clear warning to me of what was happening, but denial is a powerful drug.

I accepted all the evenings he continued to spend with his fraternity brothers as necessary to his education- al goals. I ignored the signs, and remained certain that everything was fine with us. Even the day that Terry left, six months later, I told myself that it was only a separa- tion, and that soon we would be back together. Despite our earlier uncertainties, I was sure we had become a family, and it didn't make sense that a family would sep- arate permanently. Though I had thought it would be a mistake to "trap" Terry with news of a baby, the fact that we had been a family all this time made it inconceivable to me that he would choose to live outside that family for any length of time. For a week, Shane asked for his dad every night when I put him to bed. Then he stopped asking for his dad, and asked for the dog instead.

CHAPTER 3
Lost

1970		1976		July, 1982		1987		*Now*
		Chapter 3						

During the weeks and months that followed the day Terry moved away from us, I really struggled with my unwillingness to accept that our marriage could be ending. My difficulty wasn't confined to the emotional aspects of being alone: during the years I had been with Terry, he had become the decision-maker in the relationship. My independent nature, which had been nurtured through my childhood and teens, had been replaced by a subservience that is hard for me to imagine today. As I fought the increasing emotional stress, I also found that I was afraid to live by myself. I had gone directly from my parents' home to my first home with Terry, and I had never lived alone or been in charge of a household. The combination of the emotional turmoil and the fears of being alone, even overnight, were devastating and debilitating.

I bargained with Terry. I told him I would change and be whoever he wanted me to be, but he said he didn't want the responsibility of a wife and child. I tried to make him see that he still loved me, but he assured me he did not. I reminded him of all that we had, and he told me I was mistaken. I had failed. I couldn't sustain the one thing that made me who I thought I should be – a wife. I was a failure, and I couldn't fix it. I wasn't interesting enough, desirable enough, attractive enough, witty enough; I was not an acceptable spouse. Everyone would look at me and know that I was a dud, a cast-off, someone to be dumped and discarded. They would know that something was wrong with me.

Today I can acknowledge that the failure wasn't about me not succeeding in the role of wife, and it also was not about blame or fault. Two people work to make a marriage great, and two people contribute to the breakdown of that effort. The failure of our marriage wasn't to be blamed on either, or both, of us failing to follow some predetermined "how to" list of what was required of our roles; rather, the failure occurred because we could not build mutual respect and support for each other's fulfillment. We were too immature to realize prior to our marriage how difficult that task would be. When confronted with the difficulty, we placed disparate values on accomplishing the task.

Today I can understand that the role of a spouse has nothing to do with making myself into what I think is someone's image of what I should be, but really has everything to do with developing a dedication to continued growth and commitment. However, when I couldn't fix what I perceived to be my failures in the role I thought defined me, I also could not cope with a lifetime of being broken.

I remember as a child sometimes hearing the adults talk about someone who had had a "nervous breakdown." Not knowing exactly what that meant, the image in my mind was of someone shaking, trembling, frightened and sitting alone in a darkened room. As a child and young adult, I had never heard of "depression" – at least, not in the clinical sense. People were sometimes depressed, sad, or angry. Situations could be depressing. Someone could be filled with despair. But "depression" was something that had happened in the 1930s, when everyone was poor and didn't have much to eat. Unfamiliar with the medical definition of depression, I was unable to recognize what was happening to me.

What happened was that Terry moved on to a new future, while I, emotionally beaten, just somehow got … lost.

I couldn't move forward because my mind insisted that the impending divorce was like a dropped stitch in knitting. Have you ever seen a knitted afghan that had an error somewhere in the middle? Once you have completed the first several rows, a dropped or incorrect stitch can't be fixed later – it's permanent. No matter how beautiful the rest of the afghan may be, the dropped stitch is there to stay for the life of the afghan.

I saw the end of my marriage as a dropped stitch, a *permanent flaw* in the tapestry of my life. Marriage isn't supposed to end – it's eternal. And if it ends, it must never have really existed because marriage can't end. Round and round the logic went. No matter how I tried,

I couldn't get past that mental unending loop.

I've heard it said that Alzheimer's disease is a thief that comes back every night to steal from the same person. Depression is like that. Every day, it took away aspects of my reality and a portion of the light. And I didn't see it happening, not until much had been stolen from me.

✸✸✸

The days after Terry left were filled with confusion. In many ways, I lost four months of my life because during that time I lived in a different dimension and faced demons I didn't understand. I was forced to acknowledge that this separation wasn't going to end anytime soon – possibly not at all – but I still couldn't understand why. As I was forced to face that we were no longer a couple, I discovered I no longer knew how to be an individual. As I was forced to accept that I could do nothing to prevent a "dissolution of marriage decree" from being awarded, I agonized to understand how it could be so legally simple to end a marriage.

During this time, I experienced little breaks with reality and short gaps in memory, and I had no clue what was happening to me. What is amazing is that I hid it so well from the world. My friends knew I was depressed, and my family knew I wasn't very talkative. In fact, my sisters took turns calling me once a week just to maintain some kind of connection. They all lived far away – the closest was two hundred miles.

During the day, as I attended classes and went to work, people had no idea about the different being inside me, one that took over when I was home and after Shane was in bed. I think it's similar to some alcoholics, who function normally at work, only to go home every night and drink themselves into oblivion. I wore a mask during the day, and underneath it, I wasn't any healthier than I was at night when no one could see me.

Do we hide so that no one will know and feel sorry for us, or do we hide because it's just part of being in a dark place?

***

Dark places. I have been afraid of the dark much of my life. There is the bedroom, after you shut off the light. The basement or attic, especially at night. The walk home after a movie, or a path through the trees. But there is no place so dark as that of an empty soul. There is no place so dark as the sight of the light dwindling into nothingness.

I came to live in the bottom of a well of narrow diameter; at the top of the well was a circle of light that started to shrink a bit each day. I knew the light was disappearing, and I tried not to think what would happen the day the circle closed entirely, and the last pinpoint of light disappeared forever. I knew there was a danger in the darkness, yet its icy fingers lulled me with the promise of peace, and reasons to resist became elusive. There was a need to belong to the darkness, even as I feared the loss of the light.

I thought I would suffocate under the oppression of the pain. Burning my arms became a way to push out the pain in my heart for short blinks of time, replacing it with physical pain; but the physical pain always diminished too quickly. The burns were a wall of sand, holding back the water for only a few moments before being washed away, allowing the waves of despair to reclaim their space. The waves were made of tears, and the tears just never stopped. Through blurred vision I could see instruments of death, and I so longed for some respite from the constant pain. Slowly, the circle of light grew smaller.

I carefully planned an end to it all that would not endanger my son, a way to keep him safe even as I slipped away; but when I got up during the night to execute my plan, someone had removed the means and left me without even the power to make that choice; I was angry – which drew me from my lethargy for a short time, yet the circle of light continued to grow smaller, and it was so hard to find a solution.

I abruptly ran out of class one day and drove home, suddenly certain that distance could ease the pain, that being someplace else, another town, would allow me to outrun it, to put it behind me, to vanquish it. But as I threw my clothes into a suitcase, the futility of escaping the pain by leaving town hit me as suddenly as had its promise. I surrendered to the hopelessness and waited for the darkness, and the diminishing circle of light.

✷✷✷

I awoke one night to find my not-quite-three-year-old son standing by my bed, shaking me. "Mommy yell. Mommy okay?" he asked as I tried to throw off the confusion of the nightmare so that I could help him back to bed. Night after night, the nightmares … and my son. Each night, from my place in the well, I watched what was left of the circle of light.

There was no food left in the house, and nothing for my son to eat. I stood outside the grocery store, overwhelmed by the enormous task before me. Entering the store would mean I'd have to make decisions about what to buy and what we would eat. Fear trapped me and shackled my legs, freezing me in place. But we had to have food.

In desperation I walked inside, praying that no one would speak to me, no one would notice me. The layout was familiar and surely I could find something that would sustain us until … I knew it would never get easier, and I had no way to think in terms of the future. Frantically I searched for cereal, bread, milk, macaroni and cheese. Every checkout stand had a line, and finally I was able to pay.

Air, I needed air, and safety, and I raced to the seclusion of my car. And each time this scene was repeated, I became more detached from everything around me, and more helpless to make it any better.

What I didn't know at the time was that these were all symptoms of clinical depression. I didn't gain that knowledge until years later. During the months I lived in the chasm, I thought I was crazy, and I was ashamed that I didn't have the strength to accept the loss of my marriage.

Why didn't I seek help, you may be asking. I did. Twice a week I met with a counselor who tried to guide me back to emotional health. But she never found out about the well, or the demons, because I never told her. I believed something was terribly wrong with me and I couldn't let anyone know. I was so ashamed. Nothing was real for me. The counselor, the professors, the co-workers, the friends ... the conversations were all taking place outside of me, separate, and out of my reach. I was encased in liquid – I think it was tears. The outside world was muffled and distorted, and I could not be a part of it. And it was vital that no one know. As long as I could keep it all a secret, I was – what? Safe? Insulated? Hidden. I had to stay hidden. Looking back, I ask why it was so important to be hidden, and I don't know the answer.

CHAPTER 4
Survival

1970		1976		July, 1982		1987		Now
			Chapter 4					

I can't tell you the date that marked the beginning of my recovery from that dark well after Terry and I separated. I don't know which event, or conversation, or dream, or thought precipitated the long climb back to the surface and to the light.

The moment came one night, though, when I understood that the circle of light was about to close. I could feel the walls of that dark place pressing against me, and I was greatly tempted to just let them finally enfold me forever. The thought of allowing my mind to leave – to crawl away to someplace that didn't require any coping and had no substance, a place where no one would ever see me again – offered enticing rest.

What I discovered, though, is that we are endowed with an amazing will to survive; so when faced with the certainty of that pinpoint of light leaving me alone in the darkness forever, I fought back. There truly was a single moment when my soul reached out and grabbed for the light. The next day, there were a few minutes when I could breathe and talk and attend class, minutes that weren't dominated by pain. My recovery didn't take place in a day, or even in a month, or a year. One by one, slowly, the pieces of my life had to be repaired or rebuilt. I had been taking Valium during the day to keep from hyperventilating, and then taking caffeine tablets all night to try to study. One day, I nearly dropped Shane while trying to place him in his highchair and the fear of what might have happened to him led me to stop using Valium.

My classes at the university had barely registered in my consciousness, and I was failing all of them. My counselor offered to have me excused from the semester with no penalty, but that would mean I couldn't graduate in May. I couldn't financially afford to extend my time as a student; so instead, I visited each of my professors to ask what could be done. I explained that the distractions of the divorce had preempted my class attendance and concentration, but I revealed nothing to them regarding the depths of my mental collapse. Each of them established alternative assignments to those I had missed, and I finished the semester with all passing grades. None of the assignments were minor or simple, and the hours required to complete them were most likely therapeutic.

The next semester was my last one. In an effort to put the anguish behind me, I tried to concentrate on my friends and studies. I socialized, and tried to stop wondering about Terry's new life. I made plans for my future, and decided to leave Iowa and all the sentimental ties. I searched for strength and hope and tried to find a new confidence in the individual I could be. I reclaimed my independence and found that I could make decisions just fine on my own; I learned to do my own banking and budgeting. I was living alone for the first time in my life and finally overcame my fear of the dark. I fought – and won a claim – against a credit card company that tried to ignore the Federal Fair Credit Act by refusing to give me a separate account in my own name. All that frightening and lonely time in the bottom of the well was safely tucked away so that no one would ever know it had existed.

The August after I graduated, I packed my own U-Haul trailer to tow all my belongings to Phoenix – remember, I was determined to be independent! My car was a Toyota Tercel, with approximately the engine power of two lawn mowers. The trailer weighed as much as the car! I actually knew the weight of the trailer, because I stood on a scale holding each and every one of my boxes, carefully recording the weight of each one. My friends and family who learned that I had done this thought it was really funny. But, when I rented the U-Haul trailer, a big sign inside the trailer instructed me to place two-thirds of the weight in front of the trailer axle. How could I have known how much weight was in front of the axle unless I weighed all the boxes? It never occurred to me to estimate the weight; I thought every-one weighed the individual boxes.

I set out driving to Phoenix with three-year old Shane, and our Irish setter, the two of whom shared the back seat. There were a few squabbles over who got how much space back there, but for the most part they got along just fine. Traveling with me was a young woman who was willing to take care of Shane while I drove, and who stayed with us as far as Austin. I had only one moment of panic on this first part of the trip, when my little car almost didn't make it up a steep incline with its heavy load. By the time we crested the hill, I was in first gear going five miles an hour, and wondering what I would do if the car came to a stop. This was long before cell phones, so I couldn't even call for a tow truck; and neither could I just back the car down the interstate to the bottom of the hill!

Eventually, we made it to Austin and spent a few days with my sister and her family, and from there my niece accompanied us. This second leg of the journey was a little more difficult. My little car had no air conditioning, and we were traveling in August. Figuring the trip from Austin to Phoenix would be too hot in the sunlight with only open windows to cool us, we decided to drive at night. The deer that jumped into our headlights on the interstate was surely less frightened than I was. I closed my eyes and hoped we wouldn't hit it, because I knew if I swerved I would lose control of the trailer.

Almost worse than the fear of an accident was the gas station where we stopped during the first night, and encountered a cricket invasion of horror movie proportions. There was no way I could travel any further without benefit of a restroom, but sweeping crickets off the toilet seat and hoping none jumped out of the water provided a few heart-stopping moments. Crunching with every step was no better, and the only good thing I can say for the experience is that it definitely left me wide awake and alert for driving!

Our plan was to drive all night and sleep during the day before starting out again the next evening. However, we forgot to consider the "Shane factor." He didn't need to remain awake and alert during the night, so he slept while we drove. The next morning, of course, he wanted us to play – not sleep, in our hotel room. After several hours of trying to explain that Mommy needed to rest (!), I gave up and hit the road. As a result, we arrived in Phoenix at four a.m., rather than late morning. When I called my sister to say that we would be arriving at their house in about thirty minutes, my brother-in-law suggested we park outside the gate and he would let us in when he got up the next morning. He was kidding. They let us in, showed us to our rooms, and we all went to bed.

Moving to Phoenix was the start of a new era for me, and I put those scary months and all that had happened into a secret, secluded corner in my mind, partitioned with walls and buffers, and tried not to think of what was in there. It all stayed successfully buried until that day in the car with Ruth, years later, when I read the book that allowed me to finally be free of the need to keep it hidden any longer.

CHAPTER 5
Moving Forward

1970		1976		July, 1982		1987		Now
			Chapter 5					

I chose Arizona because some of my family already was living there, enjoying the big southwestern skies and the warm climate. Don't let anyone kid you, though. Even "dry" heat is hot! It was a good time to be starting fresh, and the change of locale did provide a sense of putting away all that had torn me apart.

One morning, during the spring following my move to Phoenix, I awoke with swollen eyes, probably from a reaction to the citrus trees. I was uncomfortable, but felt well enough to join my sister and sister-in-law who were running some errands. My sister-in-law turned to me and said, "It makes me hurt to look at you! Do your eyes hurt?" I thought a minute and told her, "They don't really hurt exactly. They feel sort of ... you know how your eyes feel when you've been crying every day for a week?" The two of them looked at each other, perplexed, and both said, "No."

It was only then that I learned this experience was not a universal one, and that I should probably keep it to myself. In fact, this innocent slip, revealing something that I hadn't realized would be unfamiliar to others, raised my awareness of how careful I would have to be to keep the secret of what I had come to regard as my "crazy time".

Being a single mom in 1977 was very different than it is today. Not long after moving to Phoenix, I decided to purchase life insurance. When I asked the agent about an appropriate policy, explaining that I wasn't married but had a child, he rubbed his forehead, and said, "I know they gave us some brochures – something about policies for women who are heads of household – they must be in the closet someplace."

I also found that being a single mom with a son, as opposed to a daughter, gives rise to a few charming problems. One day my son saw me shaving my legs, and solemnly told me that when he got big he could shave his legs, too! I asked my brother to give Shane a demonstration of shaving his face, to give him an idea of what he would do when he "got big." My brother also was the one to discover that Shane had never before seen a urinal in a public restroom. Of course, that made sense, as he'd always come into the women's restrooms with me.

My new beginning in Phoenix did include dating, and through friends and family I met a series of really interesting companions during those first few years. Eventually, one tugged at my heartstrings and left me daring to imagine a long term relationship. Unfortunately, he didn't feel the same way. Alan departed from the scene, which served to magnify the low self esteem that I had developed from the divorce. Obviously, I was still a discard. I tried to see the whole episode as his loss, but I could not successfully convince myself that he hadn't left because of some lack in me.

✷✷✷

Bud and I met while working at the same company, just after I moved to Phoenix. Six months or so after my relationship with Alan ended, Bud and I transitioned from acquaintanceship to "special friends."

Most of our dates involved our four children. Shane fit by age right between Bud's older two, Kathy and Andie, with his son, Michael, being the baby of the four. Those four were a handful, and we joked that the coming years were likely to be short on tranquility if we were to continue our relationship.

Bud and I were as dissimilar as two people could be. It's quite probable that opposites do attract, but once attracted, the sparring begins! We had polar opposite methods of child rearing, budgeting, rule-setting and rule-following, and task management. During the time we dated there were only a few things on which we actually came to agree. One was that we really couldn't live without each other, and one was that our marriage would have to survive all the bumps and valleys and emotional stand-offs, because we had all our tomorrows ahead of us – and we wouldn't allow anything to change our forever.

Many people who have been through a divorce are naturally frightened by the prospect of ever facing that possibility again. That was definitely the case for Bud and me. We each had our own selfish reasons for being determined to never go through a divorce again, and we both had – possibly – matured in the time we had been single.

I will never forget the moment that I became aware for the very first time that Bud was in love with me. He was sitting on my couch, and I was working in the kitchen (not a place I feel very comfortable). I don't remember the specifics of the conversation, but suddenly, as if in a suspension of time and place, almost like those slow motion sequences in a movie, I heard him say, "I'll do it because I love you." I stopped what I was doing and just stared at him. "What?" was all I could manage when I found my voice.

"Well, you know I love you," he said, as if to imply I must be dense if I hadn't understood that. But I hadn't known. When had this happened? And how? What could he have seen in me that gave him the notion to make such an emotional commitment?

Maybe it was that I had bravely withstood his mother's admonition that just because he brought me to her house for Christmas in Colorado with all four children didn't mean that he was going to marry me (she and I later enjoyed a warm relationship when she realized I was there for keeps). Or maybe it was because I had gone to one of his desert job sites and not been afraid to get dirty and sweaty. Whatever it was, something had changed in the nearly two years we had been dating, and love had snuck up on us without my noticing.

A month later, we were on our way some place together when Bud said he thought we ought to just get married. So we did, a few months later in a small ceremony, with our four young children as attendants, plus a best man and matron of honor.

It was six months after our wedding that I was riding in the car with Ruth, reading *The Cracker Factory*. As I read the grocery store scene, about the character's inability to shop for groceries, all the memories of those days following Terry's departure flashed through my mind. The memories had been buried for a long time, and the words in the book brought everything back.

With difficulty, I tried to put the memories all back into some sort of balance. After all, I was happily married again, I was incredibly and magnificently in love with someone who treated me as an equal, and all the other days seemed so long ago. It was as if my life with Terry really had belonged to someone else. I'd been given a second chance at happiness and it had been a long time since I had permitted any of those old memories, good or bad, to take up space in my conscious thoughts.

I had put that part of my life behind me, all that "stuff" from the past with those broken fragments of a shattered life, all the grief and isolation of long ago. But that day in the car I was, for the first time, able to share those experiences with someone else, as I explained to Ruth what it was that I had suddenly found so funny in the book I was reading.

The story told in *The Cracker Factory* offered me the first glimmer of understanding about clinical depression. It was the proverbial light bulb, illuminating for me a new comprehension of the symptoms I had experienced, such as the hallucinations and the grocery store phobia. That day, in the car, I was able to tell my sister not only about those experiences, but also about this newly discovered explanation for what had happened to me during that time so many years in the past. The book made clear to me that my experiences were not unique and they were not signs that I had lost my mind; rather, those experiences were common symptoms of clinical depression.

CHAPTER 6
My Dad

1970		1976		July, 1982		1987		*Now*
					Chapter 6			

I have been an active church member my whole life. More importantly, I have been a believer my whole life. My faith has been the cornerstone of my life, and that cornerstone was built during my childhood. I described it best in a portion of a letter I wrote to my mother for an open house to celebrate her eightieth birthday. The celebration was held in our church, back in Iowa:

What a fitting place we have chosen for this celebration. Can there possibly be a nook or cranny of this church that has not touched our family? If I listen carefully, I can hear the sounds of Junior Lutherans: the chattering at meetings, roller skates at Twin Lakes, and car doors slamming as children rushed to sing Christmas carols. I can hear recitations of the Catechism, and teenagers giggling at Luther league. And I hear the music of choirs, organ, and piano. Surely there is not a Sunday School room here that has not witnessed the Christian education of at least one of us. There have been Lutheran Brotherhood meetings and Ladies Aid, Circle meditations, and banquets. And as I look back I can picture the Confirmations, weddings, baptisms, and of course, a funeral. And whether we were here to learn Bible stories or to eat maid-rites, to celebrate or to mourn, we have always been surrounded by the warmth of friends, by the fellowship of this hall.

I have sung in choirs since I was in the third grade, have been the organist in three different churches, held office for youth groups, taught Sunday School, accompanied the youth choir for musicals and the Christmas programs, and have never considered a life without the church.

This had not been Bud's experience. I was aware of our religious/spiritual differences when we dated, and I didn't expect Bud to change just because we got married. It never works to ask someone to be a person he is not. Though we all adapt, grow, and recognize new or different priorities, we must be the ones to initiate our own changes. So I didn't expect Bud to become a faithful church attendee, nor did I expect that I would stop attending. It was a good arrangement. The only thing I asked of Bud was that he go to church with the kids and me on Christmas Eve, which he was happy to do. The funny thing is, over the years, I found him more and more often ready to go with us when it was time for us to leave for church on Sunday mornings. Not every Sunday, mind you, but far more often than once each year. I gratefully accepted this gift from him.

✶✶✶

The first time I saw Bud enter the church alone, he was coming to find me. I saw him enter the side door of the sanctuary during our choir rehearsal on a Thursday evening. This was definitely alarming, and probably indicated bad news, because he just never came to the church on his own. He was still too uncomfortable to venture alone into my church world. I was right – he did come with bad news: my father was in the hospital again, but this time was not expected to live.

As soon as I got home, I contacted my Phoenix siblings. We arranged to fly to Minneapolis and drive from there to Rochester. Our sister from Texas met us in Minneapolis, and our sister from Iowa was already at the hospital with Mom. It was November and bitterly cold in Minnesota. The road signs were so heavily covered with snow and ice that we missed our turn-off at one point. The drive to Rochester was long, and filled with tension and apprehension.

We arrived late on Friday evening, joining Mom and Joyce at the hospital to hear the most recent update on Dad's condition. The doctors weren't sure what was wrong, but they knew that his lungs were filled with "gunk", so he was in intensive care. During the next few days, the doctors put him on a respirator to try to get some oxygen to his tissues; they also had to give him a nerve block because his body was fighting the respirator. He couldn't talk or see us, but he could hear us so we continued to talk to him. Once the block wore off, he could follow us with his eyes, and write notes to us on a pad of paper.

Miraculously, his condition improved to the point that he was removed from the respirator, and he could sit in a chair rather than lying in bed. We were so relieved and so grateful to have him on the mend. The four of us who had traveled from Texas and Arizona said our good-byes, kissed Dad and Mom and Joyce, and headed back to Minneapolis and our homes.

It was only about ten days later that we were called back to Rochester, about a week before Thanksgiving. Dad's recovery hadn't sustained, and once again we wait-ed long hours in the intensive care waiting room for our five minutes of visiting time each hour. A few days after we arrived, he was again placed on the respirator, and again he needed a nerve block to prevent resistance to it. Once again, we sat by his bed and talked to him, hoping he could hear us as we waited for the effects of the nerve block to diminish.

The day before Thanksgiving, one of my sisters found a coloring contest in the local newspaper – a large turkey with Thanksgiving decorations all around it. We bought some crayons and produced a masterpiece for the waiting room. On Thanksgiving Day, we went to a restaurant for dinner – something none of us had experienced on a hol-iday. The food was plentiful and delicious, and we enjoyed the short respite from the sadness of the waiting room. We weren't the only family in the waiting room, and the others' stories were heart-breaking. This little band of families, unknown to each other until tragic events gathered us into the same room – whether for an hour, or a day, or a week – became a source of comfort to each other, as we shared a common bond of emotional struggle.

Though my siblings and I had gathered there because of a family crisis, the time we spent together was a rare and incredible blessing. It is unusual in this busy world for adult siblings to have hours and hours available to talk, listen, and support – with no meals to cook, no errands to run, no offices to visit. Though we had always been close, we hadn't had the opportunity to know each others' hopes, dreams, fears, and strengths so clearly as we did that week. When one of us faltered, another was there to lend a hand, until it was that one's turn to succumb to the sorrow.

At times our mother comforted us, while in other moments she had the five of us to offer comfort to her. That Thanksgiving Day marked the beginning of the end of our vigil. When the nerve block wore off this time, Dad didn't open his eyes. His body was still alive, but by the next day we knew he was no longer with us. We could all feel the change – the absence of his spirit. Within a few days, his journey on earth ended. We had spent a week together, willing him to recover, finally recognizing it wasn't within our power to do so, and ultimately relinquishing our life with Dad.

CHAPTER 7
Tie Bucking

1970		1976		July, 1982		1987		Now
				Chapter 7				

My life with Bud was somewhat unpredictable and wild. He liked to describe himself as "crude, rude, and obnoxious", and I can attest to his ability to be just that. He liked women, and flirted outrageously; I couldn't believe he had chosen me, from all those women, to be his life-mate. In those days, we both had quite volatile tempers, so we had our share of heated confrontations. Neither of us ever backed down when challenged, though Bud was always the first one to later find a compromise.

Before Bud and I started dating, he and his brother had started a company called Western Wood Industries. This company's primary line of work was contracts with railroads to remove the cast-aside used railroad ties after the ties had been replaced with new ones. The replacement is quite an operation. The railroad crew uses a machine called a "tie handler" that pulls up the spikes from the ties to be replaced, then uses a long mechanical arm to push out the old tie and insert a new tie under the rail. The machine drives in new spikes and there is a brand new railroad tie on the line.

The railroads then offer to the highest bidder a contract to pick up the used ties and clean up all the debris left in the wake of the tie handler. There were a number of companies such as ours, and all of them bid on the contracts. The successful bidder would then "harvest" the ties, and sell them. Western Wood Industries sold most of its railroad ties wholesale to retail companies. We also had our own retail outlet where we sold directly to homeowners for landscaping or wholesale to landscaping companies. Eventually, Bud and I bought out his brother, and continued the company's adventures.

The best used railroad ties come from dry climates, because the ties have less rot. Dry climates often mean really hot temperatures, so you can imagine that "tie bucking", as we called the task of harvesting ties, is physically taxing. However, owning a company that required physical labor and the use of heavy equipment was a dream come true for me. My father had been disabled by the time I was twelve, at about the same time as my brother left for college. Suddenly, I was the one who put up the storm windows, changed the flat tires, tended the garden, mowed the lawn, and drove stakes in the ground with a sledgehammer. I loved the physical work – and an additional benefit was that my mother excused me from most of the cooking and cleaning since I did all the outside work. To this day I am far more skilled with a saw or screw driver than a stove and cookbook.

So here I was with Bud, throwing railroad ties into pickup beds, operating a Cat920 front end loader fitted with long "forks" for picking up bundles of railroad ties, driving an 18-wheeler (only on private roads – no public highways!) and working outdoors every day of the year. And Bud never doubted that I could handle these tasks; his confidence in me was a gift far more valuable than he could have known.

✶✶✶

There are many advantages to owning your own business. One is that you can schedule vacations on your own terms. One disadvantage is that you never have time for a vacation. Another advantage is that you answer to no one – well, almost no one. Our job sites were never very close to home, so to come home for the weekend, Bud had a long drive ahead of him if he wasn't able to fly commercially. When faced with a long drive and only a few days to be home, he did what most people would do: he developed a lead foot and therefore, was frequently ticketed for speeding.

One day, I got a call from our insurance agent, who told me that Bud would no longer be covered as a driver on our business vehicle insurance policy. "Well," the agent chuckled, "the insurance company can't actually refuse coverage to the business owner, but they have asked that he put his foot on a diet!" It seems business owners do answer to the insurance companies. One ticket later, Bud was notified by the state that his license was going to be revoked unless he attended twenty-four hours of driving school, so he attended the classes. The eight points on his license went away, and our insurance company was happy again. This, of course, was not a long term solution. It would only take a few years for Bud to accrue those points again. However, Bud had a better solution. He decided to get a pilot's license, bought a Cessna 210, and never again got a speeding ticket. Problem solved.

I hated that airplane, but Bud loved to fly and I couldn't help but be happy for him. He was able to get home more easily, and have more time with the kids and me once he arrived. When the children were flying with him, he loved to let one of them "take the stick", especially if I wasn't along to chide him for it. Sasha, our Irish setter, normally so hyperactive, would zonk out as soon as we left the ground, and sleep the whole time we were in the air. I swear she watched the ground disappear below us, and then enjoyed the motion of the plane.

The intensity of the hot atmosphere in Arizona creates "thermals", a whirling downdraft of air similar to water going down a drain. When small planes hit these, the plane suddenly drops hundreds of feet. Usually, our heads would hit the ceiling, and one time I happened to be glancing into the back seat just in time to see Sasha completely lift into the air with the thermal. She didn't even open her eyes!

Not a particularly good flier, I was never very relaxed in the plane. One weekend Bud and I, together with Jerry and his wife, flew to Texas to see the brothers' mom. Jerry was also a pilot, so they shared the controls. As we headed east, I noticed some really threatening weather ahead of us. I looked around and realized that the other three, including Bud, who was piloting at the moment, were all reading!

I said, "Isn't anyone other than me a little concerned about all those storm clouds directly ahead of us?" They all sort of ignored me, though Bud did answer something about not flying through them. He was right – we didn't. But when we left Texas to come back to Phoenix, the strong crosswinds on the small private runway made the take-off a harrowing experience for all of us. The others took it in stride, but I rode in a state of panic all the way home.

Sometimes, when Bud was a little late arriving from a job site, I would naturally get worried about what might have happened to him in that plane. He would then arrive safe and sound. Upon hearing me say that I had been worried, his favorite response was "I'm not going to crash and burn – that sounds like it would hurt!" And to his credit, he was always a meticulous pilot. I've known private pilots who skip some of the steps, but Bud was always very thorough in following his pre-flight checklist.

✳✳✳

Our crews had to work really hard on the job sites. Four guys would walk along the railroad tracks, working in pairs. Two guys would pick up a railroad tie and toss it onto the forks of the loader, then move aside to let the other team do the same thing. They alternated until there were twenty-five ties stacked, five high and five deep, on the forks. There was a short pause in the action as the ties were bundled, and the loader operator set the bundle out of the way. It's grueling work. The top two rows of the stack are well above waist height, and they have to be lifted quite a distance. Railroad ties weigh between eighty and two hundred pounds each, depending on if they are made of oak, fir, or pine – so tossing them requires some serious physical effort.

The second major undertaking at a job site was the tie-cutting operation. Landscapers use ties in short lengths, as well as the eight- or nine-foot original lengths. We supplied two-, three-, four-, and six-foot ties, so some full-length ties had to be cut to those lengths. This was done with a trailer-mounted hydraulic-driven thirty-inch carbide-tipped blade, powered by a gas engine. One person handled the actual cutting, while the rest of the crew "fed" the saw, carried the cut ties, and stacked them. Conditions included not only heat and sweat, but sawdust was a big part of the mix, as well.

Bud and I found that we got more work per hour from the crew with one simple modification: I worked with them. If you want to see a crew of guys work to full capacity, just put a woman on the crew. The part we didn't tell them was that Bud and I had signals worked out, so that if I was about to drop from exhaustion, I could signal him to call a break. That way, the guys never knew that I couldn't keep up with them. Bud protected me from ever having to admit that they had more stamina than I had. We made quite a team!

Bud had great confidence in my abilities to help him run the business, and he made sure the employees understood that we were equal partners. There was only one instance when an employee, who'd had years' more experience than I had running this type of business, was complaining to Bud about something I wanted him to do. Bud, in his typical fashion, informed the employee, "Pardner, there are only two people in this company who can fire you – and she's one of them."

Generally, though, I wasn't on the job site. I stayed at home to run the retail yard where we sold ties directly to homeowners and landscapers. Bud and I spent most business weeks apart, which is an arrangement that has certain advantages. We talked many times each day, but found that the time we had together on weekends was even more special since it was so limited.

At one point during our years of owning the business, I felt that my work had become a little stagnant: I competently operated all the equipment, did all the bookkeeping and financial reports, scheduled the trucks, and kept the retail yard staffed and operating. Any good manager could take my place, so I talked with Bud about hiring someone to replace me so I could find something more challenging to do. A few days later, Bud suggested that I take over bidding on new contracts. That would mean I'd need to travel to potential job sites to evaluate the quality of the used railroad ties, and then determine the price we should offer. He didn't want me to leave our company, so he found a way to make my work there a greater challenge.

We tried that arrangement for a while, but it wasn't really practical for me to be traveling since I had Shane at home. What was important to me, however, was the trust

Bud had placed in me and the effort he made to keep me involved. He made it clear that we had a true partnership, with shared responsibilities and equal contributions. I learned something from that gesture – I learned the true meaning of "the two shall become one." Bud gave me something I had been missing for so long – the sense of being valued and needed that was the very opposite of feeling discarded. He was the team captain who picked me first, instead of last, when choosing his roster, and I had never experienced as much confidence in myself as I did then because of how Bud viewed me. I no longer felt the need to leave our company to seek fulfillment, because Bud had made it clear that it was *our* company, and I was an integral part of it.

During a job in northern Arizona, the kids spent a few weeks of the summer with Bud, living in a mobile home near the job site. He hired a babysitter to stay with them during the day since I wasn't there. One overcast Friday, I hitched a ride in one of our tractor-trailers to spend the weekend on the job site. Along Interstate 17, we hit a patch of oiled road that was slick from rain, and the truck slid to the side of the road. We mowed down more than a hundred feet of guard rail as Steve struggled to keep the truck from plummeting over the edge into the deep ravine just a few feet beyond the guard rail. At the end of the ravine, the trailer jack-knifed and we ended up facing downward on a steep incline. It was a terrifying few minutes, but neither of us was hurt. Unfortunately, the same could not be said for the tractor-trailer, which had to be extracted with a crane and towed back to Phoenix.

I caught a ride to the nearest town, where I was eventually able to catch a Greyhound bus and get to the job site. While I was waiting for the bus, I was able to reach Bud by phone, and told him why I would be arriving late. His only comment was that I'd better get there in time to bring the payroll for the crew. He didn't ask if I was hurt. He didn't offer any sympathy for what I had just endured. I couldn't believe he was more concerned about payroll than my well-being! I later came to understand that this angry response was his standard way of expressing himself every time he had reason to worry about my safety.

As many years as we could manage to have someone cover the retail yard for me, the four kids and I all spent six to eight weeks during the summer with Bud on the job site. During the school year, Bud's three were only with us every other weekend, but during the summer they spent two months with us, and went to their mother's house every other weekend.

During the summer of 1985, we were staying in the tiny town of Amboy, California – population *seven*. The only businesses were Buster's restaurant/gas station and his hotel. Water had to be trucked into town because there was no local source. The temperature was about one hundred twenty degrees by eight in the morning, and there was no TV reception. The nearest large grocery store was fifty miles away. We lived in Amboy, in a three bedroom house, for six weeks with four kids and two dogs. One weekend we lost power, and we slept under damp towels to try to stay cool. During that summer, the kids and I watched movies, put together jigsaw puzzles, played games, made a weekly trip to the grocery store, and enjoyed all kinds of crafts. It was the best summer of my life.

Life with Bud was a little outside the ordinary, considering our lifestyle and occupation, but those first years were happy and exciting ones. Then came the fall of 1985, and a series of misfortunes cast the business into a dismal spiral. Financial ruin seemed to lurk beyond every curve in the road, and we struggled to hold onto the company we had built, literally, with our own sweat. We struggled together – long nights of worrying and planning and calculating. There were long days of work and fatigue and stubborn dreams – all shared, carried on four shoulders, not just two.

Facing despair when you have someone beside you, looking in the same direction and confronting the same demons, is so different from doing so if the one you most need by your side is the one who released the demons in the first place.

CHAPTER 8
Life Adjustments

1970		1976		July, 1982		1987		*Now*
					Chapter 8			

I believe that as a result of reading *The Cracker Factory*, my life was changed in many ways. A shadow only I had known to be hovering around me had vanished, and all aspects of my life became brighter and more vibrant. Though life continued to hold its share of difficulties, such as the years Bud and I struggled with our business, there was a difference in my search for solutions. Spiritually, I could sustain hope and persevere with a lighter heart and a quicker step than I had ever been able to do when facing difficulties in the years between my divorce and reading the book.

It was as if without the book, a feeling of doom penetrated every setback I encountered because I believed there was something wrong with me. With the insight and understanding I gained by reading the book, I believed instead that I had done the best I could through a difficult situation, and had eventually triumphed over my emotional fears. This realization gave me new confidence in my problem-solving abilities.

During the first five years of my marriage to Bud, I learned that he, too, had an interesting way of dealing with emotional fears. Unfortunately, I had a number of health problems during those years, and it took me a while to understand that Bud always picked a fight with me when he was worried about my impending surgeries. The first few times, I was bewildered by his overreaction to simple inconveniences or unimportant details: the location of my overnight bag that I would take with me to the hospital became a debate of monstrous proportions; the way the couch pillows were positioned was grounds for abandonment. These were never issues at any other time, and after the third incident of incomprehensible behavior on his part, including his reaction to the truck accident, I finally saw that he was afraid for me – and didn't have the words to express it.

I, on the other hand, was well-versed in the role of one who waits for a surgery to conclude. My dad had been in and out of hospitals as far back as I could remember. There were times that my mother would awaken me during the night and ask me to pack a bag so that I could go stay with friends while she took Dad to a hospital. When I was in junior high, my dad had five major back surgeries during a span of just a few years; twice he spent months recovering in a hospital bed in our dining room. By then, I was the only one of my sisters and brother who was living at home, so Dad and I spent lots of time together. I sometimes heard him crying at night when he couldn't bear the pain; I learned to shave his face with an electric razor; I visited him in the hospital; and though he had once been an accomplished athlete, I held him up as he walked me down the aisle at my first wedding.

At other times he took care of me when I was home sick with a bug. He taught me about engines and tools. He insisted that my skirts reach at least to the ends of my fingertips with my hands at my sides. He supervised as I did the home maintenance tasks he could no longer do. And he taught me to be independent.

My bedside skills while visiting hospital-bound loved ones were put to the test when Bud suffered a freak (and never fully understood or explained) loss of a major nerve in his left arm. His first symptom was severe pain, which we later learned was caused by the fraying of the lining around that nerve. Eventually, the damage affected his ability to extend the fingers of his left hand; he could grip, but he couldn't release. His wrist drooped, and several muscles atrophied from lack of enervation.

Once when I was visiting him in the hospital while he was in tremendous pain, he threw me out of his room when I refused to sneak in extra pain medication for him. But that pain was nothing compared to what he experienced the day he first had to ask me to do the lifting while we were working on an engine, and his arm could no longer bear the weight. For a man who had always conquered any physical task, who worked outside nearly every day and was no stranger to hard labor, the acknowledgement that he could not lift a twenty-four-volt battery into place was a devastating blow. For the second time in my life, I watched a man I loved struggle to overcome the psychological adjustment necessary to face and accept his physical limitations, to let me help with tasks he thought should be his, and to know that it would always be that way.

Looking back on that time, I realize that Bud's struggle to accept his loss was not totally dissimilar to my own struggle to accept a new way of life after the loss of my first marriage. Loss is a frequent event in life, and comes in many shapes and sizes. Accepting the dropped stitch in the afghan as a change in the pattern, rather than as a flaw, is a difficult task for many of us. It is amazing to me that both my dad and Bud learned to live beyond the loss and to embrace the new pattern – perhaps not with great joy, but certainly with endurance.

CHAPTER 9

Summer Vacation

1970		1976		July, 1982		1987		Now
					Chapter 9			

The summer of 1986, I made a courageous decision to take all four kids on a vacation back to Iowa for my home town's one hundred twenty-fifth anniversary celebration. The four of them were nine, eleven, twelve, and fourteen. As they weren't toddlers and were old enough to entertain themselves, one might wonder why such as trip would require courage. The reason is that they were serious squabblers. Let any outside person threaten any one of them and the other three would jump to defend him or her. But among the four of them, the bickering was endless.

My solution was having two of them fly to Iowa, while the other two rode with me in the car; then we reversed the travel accommodations on the way back. Bud would join us in Iowa, but he couldn't be away from the job site long enough to travel with us by car. It was a shame that he couldn't make the drive with us, because he really loved spending time with the four kids. Though he was what some would describe as a workaholic during those years, he was always ready to rescue us when we needed him most. However, that dedication was definitely put to the test near the end of our trip that summer.

Kathy and Michael rode with me to Iowa, and we picked up Shane and Andie at the airport when they arrived in Des Moines. The five of us set out to visit all my old haunts and visit friends I hadn't seen in a while, before making our way to my hometown. The day of the town's big anniversary celebration, we had a great time eating watermelon and watching the parade. That evening, Bud and I let Kathy have the run of the town, secure in the knowledge that it was still a small enough town that everyone there knew everyone else, and would watch out for her. She had never experienced a small town, and enjoyed the freedom it offered. The adults socialized within the barricaded two blocks of downtown – that was the entirety of downtown – buying beer from the sidewalk refreshment stands, and dancing in the street to a live band. It was a wonderful family weekend.

When we headed back to Phoenix, Kathy and Michael flew, and Shane and Andie traveled with me in the car. Exhausted from the long week of gallivanting through Iowa, the kids slept soundly as we made our way across Kansas. As I drove down a gentle hill on a two-lane road, I watched a car waiting at a stop sign to pull onto the highway. I noticed that the driver never even turned to check for traffic to her left, which would have allowed her to see us; she was intently watching for traffic from her right, as she prepared to make a left turn onto the highway. Just as we neared the intersection, she pulled out to make her turn. With a car coming toward me in the opposite lane, and a steep ditch on my right, I had no way to avoid hitting her.

When the dust settled and we had come to a very sudden stop, Shane and Andie tried to make sense of being so rudely and painfully awakened from their deep sleep. Seeing the steam from the smashed radiator, Shane fearfully asked if the car was on fire. Both he and I had hit our seat belts so hard that we ended up with huge bruises from the straps. I asked Andie, who had been sleeping in the back seat, if she was all right, and she told me she couldn't move. I eased my way out of the car to check on her, and found that a cooler had fallen on top of her, pinning her to the seat. I was so grateful it wasn't an injury that made her temporarily immobile.

Fortunately, the driver of that oncoming car had stopped, and soon others gathered, too. Someone called an ambulance. We got to a hospital where all of us were treated and released. However, we now had no car, no luggage, and we were thirteen hundred miles from home.

The hospital allowed us to use a small family room that had a phone, and I first called my sister who lived only an hour away in Missouri. She said she would come to get us so we could stay at her house for the night, and we then planned to fly home the next day. I called my sister in Phoenix and asked her to contact my insurance company, and more importantly, to reach Bud, who was by this time back on the job site. She later told me that when she reached him on his mobile phone (an early model that far predated contemporary cell phones), she said to him, "I have something to tell you but there's a happy ending!"

Bud said, "Let me pull over to the side of the road." Upon hearing the news of our accident and our totaled out car, he said "I'll go get them." My sweet husband's first response was that he would travel to Kansas from California to rescue us. Of course, that would have taken far too long to be practical, but his immediate concern for seeing us safely home was such a genuine, loving response.

Though the accident was memorable, the summer held in store for us a far more significant event.

Before Bud and I married, he told me about his older son, Gary, whom he hadn't seen since Gary's infancy. Gary's mother had wished to raise him as Gary's stepfather's son, and Bud had always honored her request.

During the spring of 1986, I suggested to Bud that since Gary was twenty-one, it might be an appropriate time to let Bud's other three children know of their brother, and to allow Gary the option of meeting our family.

Through Bud's stepmother we contacted Gary's maternal grandparents, who gave Gary a letter from me. Several weeks later Gary called me, and we arranged for him to visit Arizona over the Fourth of July weekend.

I picked up Gary and his friend at the airport, and we drove to a restaurant where Bud met us. It was the beginning of a heart-warming weekend that changed the lives of all of us, forever.

The rest of that summer was pretty uneventful by

comparison. The kids and I were able to live with Bud in Oceanside, in a beautiful condo by the beach, until it was time for school to begin in the fall.

Bud loved spending time with the kids – our four youngsters were the greatest entertainment he could imagine. We often went camping lakeside or in the woods. One Memorial Day weekend, Bud turned blue because he stayed in the cold lake water too long while patiently teaching all the children to water ski. He took the kids to the desert to launch toy rockets and to ride their mini-motorcycle. We spent many hours as a family around the TV, playing Atari. And he loved to have them on the job site with him, riding the big equipment.

A child at heart himself, and being a "weekend Dad" to the three who were living with their mom during the school year, he tended to spoil them. This included my son – not just his three. The art of maintaining impartiality as a stepparent is rare, but Bud seemed to be a natural. However, his literal lack of rules and his preference to allow them all to run amuck was a continuous source of friction between us. Though I believed that some movies were simply inappropriate for young children, Bud preferred to have them watch just about anything and then conspired with them to keep it a secret from me. I was the one who told them not to run with a stick in their hand, while Bud liked to have them drive before they could see over the steering wheel. He was also creatively playful, which I couldn't help but admire. For instance, while I insisted that the children try a bite of every dish being served for a meal, Bud used butter brickle ice cream to make macaroni and cheese when he didn't have any milk. He always won the fun award, and I was always the one to nag about bedtime and behaving properly.

That fall of 1986, despite the financial struggles of the business, we had decided we really needed a bigger house that was closer to where Kathy, Andie, and Michael lived with their mother. I found the perfect house, and we bought it without Bud even having a chance to see it. We were really excited about this new house: the kids had bigger bedrooms, and Kathy and Andie each had their own room; there was a pool and so much more space than our first little house had provided. Of course, moving is a significant undertaking – so, along with working longer hours to get Western Wood Industries back on firm financial footing, our candles were definitely burning short. Tempers were high, rest was in short supply, and time to relax grew more elusive. We both became acquainted with the uglier sides of each other.

Probably the worst episode we experienced was the night that Bud was flying home the evening of his birthday. There was some work I wanted done before he arrived so that I would have the rest of the evening free to be with Bud. To save time, I asked one of our employees to pick up Bud from the local airport where he would be landing. At the last minute, Steve called to say he couldn't get there, and hoped I would be able to go instead. With this late start, Bud was left standing there beside the airplane, alone and tired, and that wasn't exactly what he had in mind for his birthday. He was sarcastic and angry; I was defensive and melodramatic. He drove us home, dropped me off and said he was going to his ex-wife's house, where someone would care that it was his birthday. I interpreted that to mean he was wondering why he had ever allowed his previous family to slip away and that he was sorry he ended up stuck with his new family. It was such a hurtful night for both of us.

Even the most loving of relationships can stumble, leaving us confused and hurt. When those times come along, just getting up each day to manage your responsibilities is about the only thing you can do. Place one foot in front of the other, handle one crisis at a time, and look up once in a while to remind yourself that the sun still rises in the future.

CHAPTER 10

How Did We Get Here?

1970		1976		July, 1982			1987		Now
						Chapter 10			

Two days after Bud's birthday, I had surgery to repair an injury sustained in the previous summer's car accident. Though concern for yet another of my surgeries may have contributed to our painful birthday evening, I think there was much more to it than that. We were just too tired to dedicate energy to our relationship. We didn't talk much about what we had said in anger that night, but we also didn't completely put it behind us. It remained under the surface, even as we tried to make amends by being considerate and gracious to each other.

It was unusual for there to be distance between us. Through the years of working to build Western Wood Industries, we had always remained steadfastly close. Just a few years earlier we had survived, together, a day on the job site that was stressful and frightening, and yet it had brought us closer rather than pushing us apart.

It was a day that would be set apart from all others. Though the job site life of a tie-bucker is not an easy one, most of the days were pretty mundane, consisting of sweat and exertion, and following some routine. This special day, late one summer, started with a loader that needed some work done to the forks, so it had to be "roaded" into town. This meant driving a huge front-end loader along the interstate. The challenge with driving this loader was its tendency to "gallop" if the speed got a little too high. We used articulating loaders, on which the back portion pivots at the point where it connects to the front portion. The design allows for greater maneuverability, which is often crucial in off-road tight places such as our job sites often were. This particular loader was inclined to bounce a bit at higher speeds (such as thirty-five miles per hour), and the front didn't bounce in sync with the back, so it moved with a sort of galloping gait. It was my job to road the loader into town, and as cars passed me, the occupants were noticeably amused. Many waved, but some only pointed and laughed, and I was relieved to reach my destination and end my stint as the road entertainment.

When that task was done, we headed back to the job site and I was assigned to climb the signal platform to watch for trains. This was a way to warn the crew that a train was coming so they could move themselves and the equipment off the tracks. I climbed the fifteen-foot metal ladder and perched on the metal platform, ready to signal the crew if I saw a train approaching. As I sat there, I observed that there must be a lot of electricity powering those huge signal lights, the ones that flash red as a train approaches. Well, this one was out in the boonies, miles from civilization, and they are **much** bigger up close than they appear from the safety of your car. I got to thinking about all that electricity. After all, this was a metal platform accessed by a metal ladder, neither of which is really intended to be utilized except for repairing those signal lights that are powered by megavolts of electricity.

Questions started running through my mind, such as: "Is this thing grounded? When a train comes, and this signal starts flashing lights, is the electricity going to travel through all this metal? Will the jolt knock me off the platform and onto the tracks, into the path of the train? Will I break my leg as I fall and be unable to run to safety?" That was it. I scampered down the ladder and walked the half mile to catch up to the crew, informing Bud that he could watch for trains himself.

My next assignment was to wander through the tall dead grass along the tracks to find discarded metal bands that came from the bundles of new ties the railroad crew had inserted into the tracks. "Okay," I thought, "I can walk through the grass and pick up bands." I was fine until I realized I was walking where the rattlesnakes lived. Traipsing along disturbing the rattlesnakes was probably not the safest job in the world ... and so ended another of my assigned tasks.

As the morning grew hotter, and lunchtime was approaching, Bud decided we needed to check out a new access road a railroad employee had described to him. We jumped into the pick-up and made our way back to the highway, which ran roughly parallel to the railroad tracks, about five or six miles to the south. Perpendicular to the tracks and the highway, about twenty miles apart, were two small roads that connected the tracks to the highway. These small roads, separated by twenty miles, were the only two ways to access the tracks from the highway in that area, which meant a long haul back to the highway if you were bundling ties along the tracks five to ten miles into the distance between the two access roads. Bud had been told there was an old road connecting the highway to the tracks, located roughly half way between the two main access roads; it was rough, but could be used by our specialized off-road vehicles to reach the tracks. Bud figured he could save a lot of time for the crew if we could find that road.

We found what seemed to be a turn-off from the highway, and what was at first, a narrow but decent little road through the desert. We merrily drove down the road, thrilled with our discovery, thinking how good it would be to have this additional path for access, and con-gratulating ourselves for being so clever. The celebration ended along with the road, as we drove straight into a sandy creek bed and got stuck in the sand. Not easily ruf-fled, Bud let some air out of the back tires to give us more traction in the sand. Unfortunately, the stem on one tire broke and the tire quickly went flat. Grabbing the spare tire, Bud mumbled a bit as he opened the toolbox in the pickup bed to retrieve the jack. There was no jack. Evidently, one of the crew members had borrowed it.

Reasoning that we couldn't be too far from the tracks by now, we started walking across the desert in that direction. We had each lived in the desert for many, many years, and knew the first rule of living in a desert: **never** go anywhere without taking along water. We virtually never traveled without water, yet we had none on that day. There was not a drop of drinking water in the pickup to take with us. But we didn't let that stop us; we walked and we walked and we walked. It was impossible to use the sun to guide us, because it was late morning and the sun was nearly directly overhead. Every hill and gully looked just the same, and for as far as we could see, there was nothing but desert. We weren't technically lost, because we knew we were bound on all sides – by the highway on one, two legitimate access roads on two others, and the tracks on the last side. Knowing we were somewhere within that approximately one-hundred square miles was only somewhat comforting. I later thought about those old movies where the cowboys got stranded and had to walk through the desert, and remembered they always started staggering at some point. That day in the desert, Bud and I learned that you actually do stagger when lost – or, technically "not lost" – in the desert. Maybe it has something to do with dehydration of your muscles. Whatever the physiological cause, after hours of walking, we were definitely qualified for the cowboy movies.

Neither of us wanted to mention the incredible thirst we were experiencing, nor the fear that was creeping up our spines. We were probably walking in circles, and we realized that possibility as we headed in what we hoped was the right direction. We saw snake tracks everywhere. We joked about who should walk in the lead, and what we would do if one of us was bitten. We held hands, and didn't quarrel about which direction to try. We talked about the crew, and the missing jack, and what we would have for dinner that night ... but we didn't talk about water. We talked until we were too tired to talk, and could concentrate only on taking the next small step.

Four nearly four hours, Bud and I climbed hill after hill, always hoping to see something other than just another stretch of desert before us. Finally we spotted the railroad crew.

Again, we could have been ripped right from an old Western, as we staggered and stumbled down the hill heading to the water drum, and collapsing against it. Never had anything tasted so pure, so fulfilling, so life-giving as did that water. Someone from the crew finally wandered over to us to ask what had happened, and had the compassion to smile rather than to ridicule. Hydrated and cooled down, Bud set out walking the tracks to find our crew, who he figured would be only a few miles behind the railroad crew. I sat on a big rock and got comfortable for a long wait. Our plan was that Bud would find the crew, drive the loader to the pickup, change the tire, and come back to get me. Time passed, and the railroad crew quit for the day. The desert grew really quiet, and was eerily empty.

As sometimes happens in the desert, a sudden storm blew in from nowhere, and I was quickly drenched. It was better to be drenched than baked and parched – but not much. Hours passed, and I started to worry that Bud hadn't found the crew. I was terrified that something had happened and I would never see him again; I was also frightened that I would spend the night alone on that rock, and no one would find me ... until they found both of us, too late. That wasn't far from what actually happened to Bud.

After walking another several hours beyond our original trek through the desert, he became too weary to walk any further. Seeking shade, he crawled into a culvert expecting to die there. As he lay there, though, he thought he could hear the loader's engine, so he summoned the energy to climb one more hill. And there they were – our crew with their fifty-gallon water jug, which Bud apparently tried to empty before speaking a word to anyone. Then he reclaimed the jack from a penitent crew, changed the tire, and rescued me from my rock. Another day in our life as tie-buckers ended on a happy note.

I wish that I had paid more attention that day to the importance of appreciating each day we have. That day had been filled with such emotional upheaval – fear, vulnerability, helplessness, and relief. The strength Bud and I shared was a treasure, and I'm not sure we recognized how very fortunate we were that day: fortunate to survive and remarkably fortunate to have fought the battle together, side by side.

CHAPTER 11
Anniversary Celebration

1970		1976		July, 1982		1987		Now
					Chapter 11			

Working side by side had accurately described our entire marriage; so the night of Bud's birthday, when the tensions and fatigue had led us to be so hurtful, was a battle more frightening than the endless desert had been. Wary of an eroding relationship, we tried really hard to prevent the distance from widening, though we didn't seem able to close it. We tried to look ahead, and not dwell on our past difficulties.

Thanksgiving weekend, about a month after Bud's birthday, was our next opportunity to spend time with Gary. Bud and Gary had those precious days to continue building a sense of family, as they learned more about each other. They had lots of catching up to do, and it was fun watching them watch each other, as they checked for characteristics they might have in common.

As the Christmas season approached, we were looking forward to our fifth anniversary. We had carefully chosen our wedding date to satisfy a myriad of requirements. We wanted to schedule it during the holidays, so that our siblings could come from Colorado, Wyoming,

Washington D.C., Iowa, and Texas. December 27th had been my first wedding date, and December 22nd had been Bud's previous anniversary, so those two dates were not available. We finally chose December 28th, even though it fell on a Monday. A few days after our wedding we went to Hawaii for our honeymoon.

We decided it would be romantic to celebrate our fifth anniversary in that same resort in Hawaii, and now looked forward to a week of relaxing in the island sun. Shane would be with his dad for two weeks; Kathy, Andie, and Michael were with their mom; our retail manager was watching Western Wood Industries for us; everything had come together to allow us to travel. The trip had been planned twice before, but both those times we had canceled – funds had been too limited – but this time, we knew we couldn't afford to cancel again. This time, we needed the chance to close the distance between us.

Starting with our first Christmas together in 1979, we had alternated Christmas celebrations between Arizona with my family and Colorado with Bud's family. That was the year for us to be in Colorado with Bud's mother and siblings, so we first packed our bags with heavy coats and sweaters and enjoyed a snowy visit. Christmas morning was memorable as we prepared our biscuits and gravy with a holiday twist: we had **red** biscuits and **green** gravy. That afternoon we waved goodbye to Bud's family, boarded our plane, and spent just enough hours in Phoenix to unpack our bags and repack them with beach attire.

Our romantic vacation in Hawaii started out a bit rocky, as we were still struggling from the difficulties of the last year and the tensions of the last few months; we were nearing an emotional breaking point by the time we reached the surf. After a few thoughtless comments about divorce, followed by many hours of rest, contemplation, and quiet, we reaffirmed that nothing would ever drive us apart. All the anxiety generated during the previous months as we worked to recover from the devastating business setbacks, all the stress from watching each other labor to exhaustion, and all the unkind words that had flowed from dispirited hearts – all these were stripped away, cast into the ocean breeze, and forgotten in the infinity of the horizon. That week was a renewal in so many ways. We came home rested, wrapped in the warmth of sun and soul, riding a wave of optimism, and so very much in love. Fortunately, there are times in life when everything comes together, giving us the opportunity to gain perspective and to appreciate all our blessings.

CHAPTER 12

Changes

1970		1976		July, 1982		1987		Now
					Chapter 12			

Arriving home again, our day-to-day routines seemed unfamiliar and required some adjustment. With a sigh I took our films to the drug store to be processed, hoping we had some pictures that would fully capture the beauty of the islands and the laughter in our hearts.

Bud took the four kids to see the movie "An American Tale" on Sunday afternoon. I stayed home to rest and do laundry, and to avoid being the parent who would constantly be asking them to behave! Monday morning Bud flew back to California and the job site and I started the day at our retail store.

A day of work in the retail yard was much simpler than the days on the job site. We, of course, had an actual bathroom on site and fast-food restaurants only minutes away. We had no concerns about oncoming trains or being lost in the desert!

There had been a lot for me to learn in managing a retail railroad tie yard. One job I encountered on my very first day was opening a bundle of ties. A bundle is a stack of twenty-five ties, five wide and five high, bound by a metal band around the center of the stack. The metal strap is tightened with a "bander", a ratchet-type of tool that pulls one end of the metal band against the other, somewhat like buckling a belt around your waist. A clip is then placed over the two ends of the band where they overlap and is crimped with another tool, thus keeping the band tautly in place. To open the bundle, a large wire-cutter type of tool is used to cut the band, usually resulting in the ties falling into a pile. There is a great deal of tension on the band, and when released, it can easily slice through any skin that happens to be in its path. The ties weigh anywhere between eighty and two hundred pounds each, depending on the type of wood.

Anxious to prove my labor capability that first day, I jumped onto the top of a bundle and cut the band. Not only was my face directly above the spot where I snipped the band, but I was **on top** of a stack of ties that was about to fall into a heap. I know I must have resembled a cartoon character sawing off the branch on which he's sitting. This was just one of many mishaps I experienced. I had a lot to learn – but learn I did. In fact, I became a skilled equipment operator, and thought nothing of loading and unloading the loads of ties arriving by tractor-trailer from the job site.

One of my brothers-in-law was a long-haul truck driver. One day as he ate lunch at the counter in a truck stop someplace in the West, another truck driver was swapping stories with him. The other guy said he had just the other day pulled into a business yard to have his truck unloaded, and a little blonde came running out, jumped on the loader, and started unloading the shipment of railroad ties. My brother-in-law said "Wait a minute! Was this in Chandler, Arizona? If so, you watch what you say next, because that's my sister-in-law you're talking about!"

All this took place in the 1980s, and though women had come a long way in their bid to be considered equals, at Western Wood we still had many customers who just couldn't stand to see me working with the guys. One disgruntled customer asked just what I thought I was doing, and why didn't I get a college education so that I could do something other than manual labor? I proudly informed him that I did have a college degree, that I had chosen to do this work, that it was honest, healthy work, and that I co-owned the place!

Yet even though I was pretty much just "one of the guys" in the yard or on a job site, I still indulged myself with whims that are stereotypically more often associated with females. One was my love of soap operas. *One Life to Live* was my favorite, and Bud insisted that I put a TV in my office so that I could watch my soap when I got the chance. It wasn't just my soap that I watched, though. I was glued to the TV the day the Challenger lifted off, and I watched in horror as it disappeared. Our state suffered through an impeachment trial, and I also watched the unfolding of that saga. But it was only my soap that I watched with any kind of routine. I was so hooked on it that sometimes I became really annoyed if a customer called, or came into the yard to buy something during that hour. I finally got wise and decided to schedule someone else to cover the business during that hour while I went home for lunch to watch my soap in peace.

And so it happened that I was home for lunchtime, just a few days after Bud and I returned from Hawaii, when I got a call from our retail yard foreman, who said the words that ended my world: "Karen, I just got a call from Essex – Bud crashed the plane."

CHAPTER 13

Time Standing Still

1970		1976		July, 1982		1987		*Now*
						Chapter 13		

The mind is tricky, and mine valiantly blocked out the obvious. "What do you mean, 'crashed'? A bad landing? Is he hurt? Do I need to go to Needles?" I asked. Steve stalled me, saying that he didn't have any details yet, but would keep trying to find out more and let me know. I told him someone had to know the situation, and he should call the Sheriff's office while I would try the hospital. We hung up, and I called the hospital in Needles, but they had no information about a person in a plane crash. I called Steve back, and he told me that no one in the Sheriff's office knew anything.

"That's ridiculous," I said in aggravation. "They have to know. I'll call them myself." Which I did, and still learned nothing. I couldn't just stand there, wondering what to do. The walls were moving, and I could feel the tendrils of panic creeping closer. I called my brother, and asked his secretary to interrupt him in a meeting. "Bud has crashed the plane and no one will tell me what happened to him! Somebody has to know! Why won't they tell me?" Dennis took the number from me and called the Sheriff's office, but when he called me back, he hadn't learned anything either. He tried to calm me and suggested that I should not jump to any conclusions. He told me to call him as soon as I heard anything more. I called my sister, Ruth, and told her that Bud had crashed the plane and no one could tell me if he was hurt or not. She said, "I'll be right there." I called my mother, and told her that I didn't know what had happened to him. After we hung up, she packed a bag and headed to my house.

I called Steve, and when he said that he still hadn't found out anything, I demanded that he do something. **"Someone has to know if Bud is all right!** I'm going to call everyone we know in Amboy and Essex, until I get an answer!" There was a pause, and Steve asked if Jerry, Bud's brother with whom he had started the company, had arrived yet. "No, he hasn't. Did you reach him? Does he know anything?" I asked Steve. Again, the pause.

"I didn't want to tell you while you're there alone – Karen, he didn't make it. Bud died in the crash – I'm so sorry," and his voice trailed away as everything inside me collapsed.

"I have to hang up now," I told Steve.

Dead? How could he be dead? We had just been on our second honeymoon. We had a business to run. "No, oh no. No, no, no. No, it isn't true," I told the room. I leaned against the wall, I crumbled, I stopped breathing, I tried to make the words go away. I heard a car door outside, and flew out the front door into Jerry's arms. "What will we do? What are we going to do?" Jerry just held me and said he didn't know.

The next few days went by in a fog familiar to anyone

who has lost someone. The notifications are so hard. My sister, who arrived shortly after Jerry, called Dennis and called our two sisters, Fran and Joyce, who lived out-of-state. My mother arrived, and would stay with me the next few weeks. Jerry called Patty, Bud's former wife, and she had to go home to tell Kathy, Andie, and Michael. Someone called our pastor, and he arrived shortly. Jerry called the hospital in Colorado where their mother had been admitted with heart problems, and Wyline (Jerry's and Bud's sister) had to break the news to her that she had lost a son, her baby. Shane arrived home from school, and I blurted out the horrible news. I called Gary, who had only been reunited with Bud the previous July; he made his third trip to Arizona the following day.

Friends and family from the local area and from all over the country arrived and filled the house with love and support. Jerry and Joe, another of Bud's brothers, took shifts staying at the house with me each hour of the day. My siblings and mother were there to help make the house ready for the friends and family who would visit; to help me make arrangements, and to answer the many phone calls.

The children and I saw Bud for the last time before the casket was closed, and hundreds attended Bud's funeral.

Stunned, I moved through the days. I was 34; my first husband had left me, my father had died, and now my new husband was dead. I just withdrew, into another secret place ... and hid it from everyone ... again.

CHAPTER 14

This New Place

1970		1976		July, 1982		1987		Now
						Chapter 14		

My life has been blessed in many ways, but probably the blessing most central and most instrumental has been my family. Despite the closeness of our family, I was unable to share my dark secret with them a second time. It was not my grief that remained a secret, for I could not hide my swollen eyes and my broken heart. My family was there for me in every way and remained steadfastly at my side as long as I needed them to be there. And for nearly a year, I moved in numbness as I grieved.

The first year following a loved one's death is, of course, filled with many firsts. The first Valentine's Day, the first birthday, the first Easter, Halloween, Thanksgiving … and the first Christmas. All these days are difficult – even more difficult than the days between them. I was so fortunate to have friends and family that just never allowed me to go through a special day without doing something to *make* it special. Despite their best efforts, though, it couldn't be the same as while Bud was alive. Yet without their efforts, I would have lacked the strength to later, once again, face the uphill climb to recovery.

Perspective is a funny thing. About three months after Bud's death, I took my vacuum cleaner to be repaired. For some reason, during the conversation with the clerk, she suggested that perhaps my husband could come back to pick up the vacuum when it was ready. I solemnly replied that I was a widow, and would take care of it myself. The clerk asked me how old I was. "What a strange question," I remember thinking. When I told her I was thirty-five, she said, "You're young! You'll find someone else." I do believe that she meant well, but it was so hurtful on that day. Just think – here it is, more than twenty years later, and I still remember even the inflection in her voice.

As time passed, there were so many good friends, who without the slightest notion they were doing something I would remember for all these years, said to me in greeting, "Hello – how are you?" It's such an innocent question, so commonly asked and rarely intended to be taken literally. Yet I often wanted to point out to them that I was not doing well at all, and wasn't it obvious that of course I wasn't doing well – how did they *think* I was doing? Good grief – my husband died. I had lost my best friend, my lover, my business partner, my fellow parent, my caregiver, my confidant – **how do you think I'm doing?**

Thankfully, I never voiced those thoughts to anyone, and I usually managed to utter the expected "Fine. How about you?" I was recently relating this story to someone, and she asked me what I would advise saying in greeting to someone who has recently experienced the loss of a loved one. It's not an easy question to answer, even for me. I usually just try to let the person know with my words that I realize this isn't an ordinary time in their lives. "Are you managing okay?" or "Is there someone to help you through the days?" tends to be how I greet those I know to be grieving. But of course, those questions may not be comforting to all who grieve. Maybe it's in my mind only that they are more helpful than a cheery "Hi – how're you doing?" would be.

In the midst of my grief, I came to resent the number of times I had to prove to some entity or government agency that my husband was dead. I had to announce it again and again, and even provide a certificate to prove it. It seemed they should just be able to take one look at me and know that I truly was a widow. And I couldn't believe how easily the world continued its normal routine. How could sporting events continue, people watch the news, and critics review new movies like normal, when my world was so very far from normal?

There were days that I shook my fist at the heavens – not to chastise God, but to chastise Bud! What was I supposed to do about the business? Did he want me to continue contracting with the railroads? Did he want me to downsize the operation? Why hadn't he told me about the informal agreement he had with one of our customers? Where were his receipts for that last month? How could he leave me with all the responsibility? How could he **leave** me? <u>I WAS SO ANGRY WITH HIM</u>.

And then I felt horribly guilty for being angry.

A sense of responsibility can be a strong foundation for a worthy life; or, it can be an unrealistic burden to carry up the mountain. During my early years of living in Phoenix, I was working multiple part time jobs to support us while I went back to college part time. One was working for a guy who had his own business doing clean-up and repair on rental properties and houses being readied for sale. One day, while preparing to repaint the interior of an empty house that was about to go on the market, I opened the drapes in a bedroom to let in more light. As I did so, I saw two human legs on the floor of a closet to my left. I uttered some muffled exclamation of shock, and bolted for the door with my heart pounding, certain with each step that hands would grab me from behind and brutally stab me to death. Gasping, I reached the door and fumbled with the knob to make my escape.

I ran down the driveway – and suddenly stopped, turned around, and ran back to the door. I had intended to get in my car and drive away, but I couldn't do that without first locking the door to the house behind me! After all, I was responsible for that house, and I couldn't just leave it unlocked! This was a case of an overactive sense of responsibility, one that could have been perilous had the "houseguest" truly been dangerous. Later, the police found the young man, who told them that he had just gone into the abandoned house to sleep off a hangover.

I wonder sometimes if we don't do the same thing with our emotional health. Is it possible that some sense of responsibility for not troubling others, for not being a burden, or for not making someone worry, is the reason we seek a secret place to hide, which in the end puts us at even greater risk? I don't know for sure, but I do know there are people out there today and every day that have experienced this same shadowy otherworld, and some of them never find a way to leave it. I know some never leave it because I read about them in the paper occasionally. They are the mothers who try to commit suicide and take their children with them; they are the parents who murder their children and don't try to conceal it. They are the people who, with loaded guns, suddenly appear in a former workplace, or commit some desperate act in an attempt to get someone to listen.

This is in no way to say that all those who commit horrible acts of violence are to be excused because they are depressed. However, I know it is possible to consider unspeakable solutions to despair, to stand at the line that separates depression from rage. Those of us who recognize the danger are able to pull back from that line and seek ways to never come near it again; others don't find a way to do that. Some of us have the love and support of family and friends – and even if they don't know how close we have come to crossing that line, their influence helps us back away from it. Others have no such people in their lives to help them back away from the line. For some of us, the realization that **not** sharing our pain is potentially far more hurtful to others than sharing it could ever be, comes in time to prevent further tragedy; others never see that truth.

***

For that first year, until Christmas, I tried to heal while staying in the isolation of depression. First, I learned to drop a curtain in my mind that shuttered the pain behind it. I could cry all the way driving to my sister's house, and then walk in with detachment for the evening. I could run Western Wood all day, making financial decisions, waiting on customers, conducting business as usual, and then go home to cry in my room all night. The secret place of depression is, by nature, isolated from all those around you. It isn't a conscious act of excluding everyone – it's just that people who aren't depressed can't visit that place. But most frightening of all, was that I couldn't even share the suffering with others who grieved: I watched my son struggle with his own grief, and coldly turned away rather than comforting him and letting him see my sorrow.

Recently, someone asked me how my children had coped with Bud's death, and it was with great sadness and regret that I had to answer "I don't know." I was so closed off, so disconnected from everyone, that I don't even know the ways in which they suffered. I could not share my suffering or notice theirs, and the failure to do so prevented healing from taking place.

The first Christmas after Bud died, my mother with all her children and grandchildren and the associated in-laws gathered together. It was quite a group. For the months following his death, I had somehow managed most of the time to go about my life as if Bud was simply away on a job site, and would be home soon. However, I couldn't pretend that something could keep him away from us for Christmas; when Christmas arrived and he didn't come home, I knew that he was not coming back. I hit that solid wall of acceptance and had a great fall. The pieces were far too scattered to be put together again.

As the second year without Bud began, I literally came to live in two different worlds, one that was outwardly sad but not obviously abnormal, and one that was completely set apart from normal life. Powerless to stop the fall, I recognized that I was slipping into another chasm. This second chasm was far deeper than the first had been; and its shape was not a well. It was vast and endless and open; there was no color in it, no birds, no music. Outside this place all those things still existed; they just weren't there for *my* eyes or ears. As the months of that second year passed, all my belief systems dissolved away, leading me to that line between depression and rage, and leaving me bitter, cynical, and without even the desire to find any hope.

One fallen piece of me felt that I finally understood God. One night, as I was leaving a counseling session with our pastor, who was also a good personal friend, he asked me if I wanted to check some of the verses in the Bible that spoke of feeling abandoned by God. I remember that in that instant I understood God with absolute clarity. I responded to the pastor, "You don't get it – I do not feel abandoned by God. _I_ – am – abandoning – God.

Though I didn't go on to explain myself, I finally realized in that moment that we are mere puppets. After all, what good does it really do to be faithful and try to follow the Commandments? Our comfort in times of sorrow is no greater than if we never followed the rules. Our suffering is not lessened by virtue of believing in God's grace. Oh, I still believed in God. I believed Him to be just like the gods of Greek mythology, sitting there on a cloud somewhere pulling the strings that jerked us around to provide His entertainment. I was finished seeing the benevolence I had always seen in the past. In fact, I was done with anything good and kind and compassionate. It wasn't just God I would abandon – it was all things in life that fell into the category of goodness. I would definitely never again lapse into a Pollyanna view of the world.

During the early part of that second year after Bud died, as I retreated more and more deeply into this desolate place, I found that this time I was even more skilled in hiding than I had been the first time depression had ruled my life. That curtain which I dropped in my mind no longer functioned to just hide the depression, it actually separated the two places of my existence. In this new hiding place behind the curtain, I didn't just feel pain – I appreciated the irony of deceiving everyone and letting them think I was not splintering into little pieces. In this place, I didn't care about anyone. The cynical and unfeeling person I had become was less cautious of flirting with that invisible line. Yet in my other world, the one where I was visible, where I talked to people and moved from day to day, I knew I could never repay the kindness directed my way. They were all trying so hard to be supportive, and I owed them so much. It wasn't fair to let them know their efforts weren't working. So I didn't ever let anything from one place cross into the other. They were always kept separate, and that was how I survived.

> *To be alone and lonely, is a loneliness of the heart.*
> *To be not alone and lonely is a loneliness of the soul.*

In high school, I found this quote, attributed to "Anonymous", and used it for a calligraphy exercise. At the time, I was going through a phase when I believed that I had come to this earth to be "alone". I felt separate from my older siblings, and when it came to friends I was just not quite "with it". I had a number of really good friends, who are close friends yet today, but I just couldn't always connect in the way I thought I should. I had been a latchkey kid long before the term was in use, long before people actually needed a house key since no one locked the door, so I had spent a lot of time on my own even as a young child. This time alone was not something I viewed as a negative; in fact, I felt just the opposite – somehow special because I was trusted to stay out of trouble and manage my simple needs until everyone got home for the day.

The memory of that quote and the feeling I'd had that

I was meant to be alone, came back to me during the time of desperate withdrawal following Bud's death. For I was not alone – I had a great support system – yet I felt a deep loneliness in my soul. I wondered if perhaps I was intended not to have men play an important role in my life; maybe, for some reason, I was not allowed to have any male be dear to me. I feared for my son, as I was sure he would be taken from me, too. I was sure my very existence was a threat to him. It would be so easy to pull into traffic and be "accidentally" broadsided. Better yet, I should make sure that Shane never felt the isolation or the pain that I was experiencing – I should make sure he wouldn't be *on earth* to know it. There were so many things I needed to do.

These were the horrific thoughts of a mind overwhelmed with despair. In hearing my own thoughts, some part of me cried out – and wept with fear. From those depths came the acknowledgement that without help, I would end up existing in one place only – it would be the dark chasm behind the curtain, the dark place that held so much despair.

So I dared to allow my lost place to cross over into my visible world only long enough to ask my pastor to refer me to someone who could help me, someone who didn't know me. I asked him to give me a name and then never speak of the conversation again.

He gave me a referral; however, the next time he saw me, he asked if I had called the therapist. His words elicited terror – the terror of having him breaching my walls. I was stunned at having someone openly acknowledge that other, secret place. Of course, he couldn't have known that his question would be a horrible shock to me – I had been so very careful to not let anyone know what was happening to me. Through the distorted space between us, I muttered an answer to his question and fled, fighting to quickly rebuild the wall and make it complete again. Just a few hours later, I felt reassured to realize how successful I had been in keeping him from understanding the depth of that separation between my two worlds.

Taking this step to reach for help was one of the most difficult things I've ever done. Somewhere in the depths of all that despair and isolation, my own voice was telling me that the chasm was something I had experienced once before – I knew this place, even though it had taken a different form this time. I also knew I would never be able to leave it without help. What I didn't know then, but can see now as I look back, is that the understanding of clinical depression that I gained from reading *The Cracker Factory* allowed me to forgive myself for all the thoughts and feelings I was experiencing. With that forgiveness came the acceptance that I was <u>worthy</u> of receiving the help I so desperately needed.

CHAPTER 15
The Long Climb

1970		1976		July, 1982		1987		Now
							Chapter 15	

My first session with the grief therapist consisted of my sitting in her office for fifty minutes, crying. I don't know what happened during the subsequent sessions, except that she gathered the pieces and reassembled them. And once I again lived in only one world, instead of two, I was able to begin to mend. It was an arduous climb, and it was not easy to face that road of recovery a second time. Probably no one but the two of us knew that she had brought my two worlds together and started me on the road that would eventually bring me peace. I trusted her with my life, and the trust was well placed.

For about three months she gently nudged me in the right direction, and helped me to find my way from that vast chasm. Sometimes she gave me homework – writing a letter to Bud, making a list of how I defined healing. Maybe what counseling does for us is provide a safe haven where we can dare to believe, if only for an hour, that it's possible for our heart to mend. In the sanctuary of my therapist's office, I could confront the vast chasm left in the wake of losing the person who I needed most during this time of sorrow, the one who had filled so many roles in my life, and who had been taken from me in the space of a single moment. I could confront the loss and allow myself to stop yearning for the impossible: I could not go back in time and change the outcome of the plane crash. There, in her office, I could stop fighting an exhausting, hopeless battle.

Today there are many forms of therapy for the depressed. I'm sure that not all methods are effective for all people, but there is help and there is more knowledge today than in the past. And today I understand that there is no shame in needing outside help. Just as there are people who can't sing, or paint, or diagnose a stuttering engine, there are people who cannot cope with grief on their own without guidance. And each of us is worthy of being helped.

Though I was beginning to heal, I wasn't anywhere close to having finished grieving. It was many years before I could think of Bud and touch the memories without shedding tears. But the bitter desperation was behind me. One day, a good friend told me that though she knew how much I was hurting, there was a peace in me that she envied. She knew it came from my faith, and she hoped she would someday feel that same peace.

I can't tell you that there was an epiphany that brought me back to that faith. The distance I had tried to put between God and me had never become all that great, because He had always remained right there beside me through all those troubled days. His presence, though, was not always so obvious to me, appearing in the guise of the angels who happened to call just when I most needed to hear a voice; or in a night of peaceful sleep after many nights of restless tossing and turning; or in the contentment that seeped into my life at odd moments.

I discovered guidance in unexpected places. One was the TV show *The Golden Girls*. From this superb comedy came words of wisdom that I have held in my heart from the time I heard them. The character Sophia was visiting a friend who had been widowed and was having trouble finding her way. The friend said to Sophia, "I'm afraid that if I let go of the grief, I won't feel anything at all." I was astounded at the insight of the person who wrote that line! It is precisely the fear you experience when you are empty inside and have only grief to fill the void. If the grief is gone, what will replace it? Will you just remain an empty void? It's a frightening thought, letting go of the only feeling you have left.

Another jolt came from a novel, the title of which I have forgotten. The line was, "Nobody loves a grieving widow." When I read that line, I instantly remembered how sad my brother had looked when he told me, "I just want to hear you laugh again." Was it possible that I was forcing all my family to endure endless hours of dreariness? Were they yearning for just one single outing that didn't include my tears? Bless them, they never let show how hard it must have been to remain patient with me during all those years.

I made a few mistakes along the way. One year on

New Year's Eve, I decided to stay up late watching a movie so that I could welcome in the New Year. The movie sounded great. It was *Out of Africa*. What I didn't know is how the movie ends, with the woman hearing her love's plane crash as he flies off on a trip. I should have guessed the ending when I learned that he was a pilot.

An evening planned to watch old family videos that, not surprisingly, would include footage of Bud sounded like fun, and I was prepared to watch him on the screen as the family sat down that evening. Everything was fine until we switched to slides, and for some reason I wasn't prepared to see Bud in the still pictures. Caught off guard, my heart was filled with sorrow, and I missed him oh, so much.

At other times, I received healing from angels unaware of their gifts. One day, out of the blue, my brother-in-law mentioned that he really missed Bud. Just hearing someone else speak of missing Bud brought me comfort. It's more natural for people to avoid speaking of the person who has died; I believe they think the reminder is painful. What they don't realize is that it is far worse to never hear the loved one mentioned, as if that person had never existed.

A good friend once observed that somehow Bud seemed to have become a saint in my memories, someone who had no flaws and had never done anything to aggravate me. She pointed out that I wasn't really doing anyone any great favors by distorting him rather than remembering him as he had been – a mortal with strengths and weaknesses. She suggested that making him into something unrealistic wasn't really honoring him. And she was right. There is nothing wrong with the person he was – I didn't have to make him into someone else.

There were countless little things, unexpected events or words that lessened the sense of loss and allowed me to remember without hurting. The smallest anchor could become a source of strength. For years I carried a hand-written copy of a verse I had read: "Those who live in our hearts can never die." Someone told me about an actress who while appearing on *The Johnny Carson Show*, had remarked that we all grieve on our own timetable. It was such a relief to me that I didn't have to conform to someone else's idea of how long was long enough. I wonder if we haven't made a mistake in dropping the custom of wearing black during a period of mourning. It was a way the grieving could say to the world, "Give me this time. Don't ask me to live as if my world is right-side up. Recognize that I am often just trying to breathe, just trying to make it through the next moment." Without that visible sign of mourning, we move about, often looking awful and appearing distracted and off balance – which we are – without people having a clue about the cause of our disarray.

The loneliness was very hard. Though I spent much time with friends and family, I was always the third or fifth wheel, and on New Year's Eve there was no special embrace reserved just for me. Bud's stepmother told me one day that after her husband had died what she missed most was the affection, the warmth that comes only through the relationship of a life-mate. It is so true. Though the loneliness was difficult to bear, I believe that it is part of the healing process; it is part of what helped me to accept the rage and the despair within my heart, because it gave me the time needed to reflect on me, rather than on my lost relationship. The loneliness is hard, but it did lessen with time.

One of the most exceptional developments of my years after Bud died was that his former wife, the mother of my three young stepchildren, shared them with me. My children were a wonderful and welcome focus in my life as I began to heal. Several times, I took Kathy, Shane, Andie, and Michael to see Gary, in Texas. We had a chance during different trips to meet several of Gary's girlfriends – and best of all, we all attended his wedding. I loved every minute of having the five of them together. Shane and I could have lost them all, along with Bud, and I am so very grateful that they are still today, my children.

Life became okay as I started to heal; it consisted of work, church activities, Mom and my siblings and their spouses, as well as the kids, and school events. The four kids kept me busy with sporting events, band and chorus concerts, and cheerleading feats; I took my turn driving them to school, Confirmation classes, and dances. I taught the youngest three to drive. Kathy, Andie and Michael were a constant source of comfort to Shane and to me; they had been a part of our lives for all the years we had known Bud, and our love for them was independent of Bud's love for them. Though their mother remained their primary caregiver as they grew to adulthood, she made it possible for them always to be part of our family. The day of Bud's death, she and I began a friendship that has deepened over the years and has resulted in the two of us becoming family, as well as close friends.

I kept Western Wood for almost two years; this included the year and a half of my deep depression. Three or four months into my recovery, when I wasn't as desperate to hide from strangers, I decided that it just wasn't fun to have Western Wood Industries without Bud. Without the recovery, I could never have withstood separating myself from the business that Bud and I had worked so hard to build together. Every day of my life with Bud had included that company, and the thought of living without it was like losing Bud a second time. It is so hard to let go of the material ties to the person for whom we grieve. For me, hanging onto that symbol of our dreams and hopes for the future was a way of feeling connected to Bud, and I felt that abandoning Western Wood was the same as abandoning Bud. I felt disloyal when I made the decision to leave the company behind and migrate to some other future; I struggled with these feelings, and had many arguments with myself.

In the end, I finally acknowledged that Western Wood would never survive with only me to run it. It had been a team effort, and I couldn't do it alone. I also couldn't bear the thought of someone else owning it, so instead of selling it I liquidated the company. I still have the sign that hung in the office and a few other mementoes. Following the last weeks of operation, I took all the employees for a weekend in Laughlin, and gave them each something from the company, tokens that represented their relationships with Bud. I put together photo albums, so that the children would always have a record of the company that had been our life all the years we were a family with Bud. I locked the gates of the retail yard for the last time, and for years could not drive by the property without crying.

With no business to run, for a while I floated around with temporary jobs, finally settling into a permanent position doing office work. A young woman, maybe seventeen or eighteen, come to work at this company for a while one summer. She was a relative of one of the company's executives, and was a little outspoken. This was about three and a half years after Bud died. One day she noticed my wedding rings and asked me something about my husband. I told her I wasn't married. Her response was, "What's the matter – did he dump you?" When I told her he had died, she had the grace to be mortified at her thoughtlessness; I hope she learned to think before speaking.

She wasn't my only experience with a young person who never considered the possibility that I was a widow. Most of us have probably played a child's prank utilizing the phone at some point in our youth. One evening, I answered the phone at home to hear a teenaged girl's voice, asking if this was Mrs. Kibler. I told her I was Mrs. Kibler. She said she was so sorry to have to tell me this, but she was having an affair with my husband, and just thought I should know. I told her I was quite certain she was **not** currently having an affair with my husband, but she continued to insist that it was true. I finally told her he had died, and how long ago. There was a long silence on her end, and then she disconnected. A childish prank that she thought would be funny; as hurtful as it was for me, I can only imagine the damage if she had reached someone who actually was experiencing marital problems.

✳✳✳

My son was home yet for five and a half years after Bud died, so I wasn't living alone. Together, we managed the house and the yard, and somehow survived his teenager years. The December that Shane was to turn sixteen, he was making a trip to Iowa to spend Christmas with his dad. Earlier that month, Sasha, the Irish setter that we had gotten as a puppy when Shane was five months old, had reached the point when she no longer could live comfortably. She was almost sixteen, and it was time to let her go. Shane said goodbye to her when we left for the airport, knowing that she wouldn't be there when he came home. He had literally never known life without her. She had been a constant in his life through all the changes and adjustments, and it was a difficult parting. Such is the case for most children and young adults when they lose a pet. But for Shane, Kathy, Andie, and Michael, during those first years after Bud died, surviving the ordeal of outliving a pet took place in a different context than for most of us. Having lost a parent while they were so young, the subsequent loss of a pet was both tragic because it was an additional loss, and yet at the same time was tolerable because it was so much less significant than losing Bud.

CHAPTER 16
Student Life

1970		1976		July, 1982		1987		*Now*
							Chapter 16	

As I contemplated my fortieth birthday during Shane's senior year of high school, I experienced an unusual midlife crisis. It occurred to me that nearly half my life was in the past, and I had never used my college degree in science. I figured that if I was ever going to work in the field, I'd better get started! Finding that no one wanted me – that they seemed to think it crazy that I thought I could do anything in the sciences after all those years of being away from it – I started a radically new phase of life: graduate school.

I have often characterized my life as a graduate student, whose fellow grad students were the same age as my children, as being one where no one understood my jokes. I received a lot of blank looks from my fellow students.

After my experience as a "returning student", as they called those of us who were older than most students, I urge any young people who want to get a post-graduate degree to do it while they are young. The stamina that is required to survive years that include teaching fifteen to twenty hours per week, attending classes and studying for exams, and also trying to accomplish research is tough to find after age forty. It can be done, and it's never too late to pursue a degree, but I know it would have been easier to do during my twenties. My mother graduated from college at age fifty-nine, after having already been a teacher for more than twenty years. I guess late degrees run in the family.

Many things happened during my years as a graduate student. I became a grandmother three times, I used the Internet daily for the first time, and I went on my first date – a blind date! – in the nine-plus years that had passed since Bud's death. By that time, I could look back and see that the nine years had gone by in approximate thirds. For three years after Bud's death, I grieved and gave little thought at all to what the future might hold for me. The next three years were a bit of an awakening, with new interest in the world around me. During years seven to nine, I sometimes considered that maybe it would be all right to date again; but I couldn't think of any good way to meet single guys my age. Then friends interceded – and thus, the blind date. The friends who orchestrated this blind date were the same pastor and his wife who had known me when I married Bud, had watched our blended family grow, and had been two of the good friends who made such a difference during those difficult years after Bud's death.

Most likely a drastic life-change such as entering graduate school is not a requisite for healing; but in many ways it helped me reconcile my feelings of guilt about enjoying life even though Bud wasn't with me anymore. I had been just floating, adrift, as the years passed, and this was a way of setting a specific course. It allowed me to see that letting go was not an act of abandonment; rather, it was just the opposite. Letting go was a way to set aside and honor a very special time in our lives that had belonged to not "me", but to "us".

Some people travel after a loss, or take up a hobby they always wanted to try; others go to graduate school. Returning to school had the effect of setting boundaries around my time with Bud, and of saying to him, "I can't re-create our time together when you aren't here. That time was special, and it should be preserved as ours, and not be continued on as 'ours without you'."

My post-graduation plan was to do my post-doctoral work in HIV research. During grad school, I'd had the opportunity to volunteer as a "Baby Buddy." These were a group of trained volunteers, sponsored by an HIV-support organization, who babysat HIV-infected/affected children. Sometimes I babysat in someone's home, and sometimes at organizational functions. One evening, I was assigned to baby-sit with children whose parents were attending a support evening that offered a variety of sessions in different categories. It just happened that no one had brought their children along that evening, so I had no babysitting to do. One of the sessions was for grief counseling, and only one participant had asked to attend that one. The session counselor asked if I would be willing to attend it as well, to make it less awkward for the one participant. I was happy to do so, and explained that I did know something about grieving.

The three of us started the session, and at one point the young participant told us her story and how she came to be attending an HIV support group session. She told us that, a few years before, on the day before her wedding, she had answered a phone call and taken a message from a doctor's office that was intended for her fiancé. During that phone call, she learned her husband-to-be was HIV positive. I cannot even begin to imagine how devastating it would be to receive such news. I believe most of us would have called off the wedding ... but this woman didn't abandon her husband and she never faltered in her love for him. She later became his nurse and took care of him through the ravages of AIDS, seeing to his needs until she watched him die at home in his own bed, where he wanted to be.

She told the story humbly, and with no thought of her own sacrifice. She had come to the support group, knowing that others would understand the months of his illness, and the brevity of their union. Two of us that evening listened to her story, and learned a lesson in love that few in this world would be qualified to teach.

CHAPTER 17

The Journey

1970		1976		July, 1982		1987		Now
								Chapter 15

I don't know anyone who has never grieved, who hasn't suffered the loss of someone or something in life – a parent, child, sibling, friend, pregnancy, spouse, marriage, career – a loss that brought them great sorrow. I have been so blessed - my life has been touched by the love and caring of so many people, who were there to help me through each loss. The same is not true for everyone. In Rockville, Maryland, where I spent four years doing post-doctoral work, I saw one day at the post office a man who I assumed was homeless. He was standing in the snow, not bothering anyone, but just standing there in socks, no shoes. No one should have to stand in the snow without shoes; I wondered what loss had brought him to be there. I tried to think of a way to get him some shoes – I was afraid to invite him into my car, and I didn't have any cash with me. I drove away without finding a solution, saddened that my inaction had provided him only further loss.

Though it has been many years now since I emerged from that second chasm, there are still moments that can bring an instant tear to my eye and ache to my heart. Years ago, as I held my first grandchild, I could hardly bear thinking about how much Bud would have loved being a grandfather. He spoiled his children in every way he could find – what a joy it would have been for him to do the same with grandchildren. When I looked into Ashleigh's eyes there in the hospital, I could see her father and her grandfather in them, and it broke my heart to not have Bud there to share the joy.

Just a few months ago, I was going through some boxes that traveled around with me through graduate school and my post-doc years. I opened a stationery box that contained some trinkets (no stationery), and among the treasures were the few remnants that I had found at the crash site: a belt loop, a piece from Bud's travel checkers game and a few other odds and ends.

There are still songs that make me sad – in a nostalgic sense, not one of despair. Healing, learning to love again, enjoying life – to experience all these things doesn't mean you ever abandon the appreciation of what has been lost.

Today I still have few answers, and have many questions. I cannot know if there is a third chasm for me and if so, what will follow it. I so ache when I see those who are grieving. If only I could, I would take the hand of each one of them, and pull them through the void to the other side where they could experience the memories without those memories being so painful; but, of course, the passage to healing is a very personal and vital one, a passage that cannot be bypassed. My belief is that there is always something yet within each of us, some as yet untapped reserve of strength; there is also a source of humor, and the capacity to appreciate the joy and delight held for us in any given moment. One of my sisters suggested once that though it would be impractical to live as if each day was our last, it might be good to behave as if we had only six months to go. We might be more likely to get our papers organized, we might travel to see the places we really want to see, we might remember to tell people how much we love them. We could probably all do with a little more appreciation for what we have in the moment.

I married Tom, the man I met on the blind date back in graduate school. It's actually amazing that we had a second date, because for two weeks after that first dinner, I didn't hear a word from him. Not one to wait in limbo too long, I decided to call him to find out his plans. I got his number from the friends who had arranged our date, and placed the call, figuring that he would be out of town anyway, since I knew he traveled a lot with his work. But he was home, and when he came to the phone I said, "Hello, this is Karen. We met on a blind date a few weeks ago, and I just wondered if you were planning to call me or if you decided that wasn't a good idea."

He laughed, and replied, "I did plan to call you, but I wrote down your name wrong, so I couldn't find your phone number." Right. Couldn't he have thought of a story better than that? Nevertheless, we did arrange to have dinner the following weekend, and as the evening progressed we chatted about this and that, just getting to know each other. Tom started telling me about the numbing experience of being in a plane that had just landed in Detroit when the Northwest flight crashed there.

I interrupted to ask if our friends had told him how my husband had died, and he got a horrified look on his face. "Not in a plane crash, I hope." I felt so sorry for him!

The evening turned out wonderfully, and we easily worked past his moment of horror. A few months into our relationship I made it clear to him that I would be graduating in a little over a year, and then moving someplace far away to take a postdoctoral position. I just didn't want him to think I had ever misled him about my plans. He seemed to be fine with the knowledge that this was not a relationship that would continue past my graduation, and so we dated merrily along through those last sixteen months or so.

Happily, by the time I moved to Maryland, we had both recognized that ending the relationship was not the answer, and we survived the next four years having to commute twenty-two hundred miles for a date. When the possibility of marriage appeared on the horizon, Tom accepted without question that I was a package deal: me and five children. Combined with his three children, we created quite a large family! On top of gaining five children, Tom, an only child, recognized that I also brought to him my four siblings and their spouses, and two complete sets of in-laws. Our wedding was on the same calendar date as had been that blind date, exactly five years later.

A few days after the wedding, I returned to my work

in Maryland, where I would be for the rest of that year. Three weeks after our wedding, Tom had a heart attack. It was a mild one – but a strong warning to him. I couldn't get a flight home from Maryland until the next day, so it was a long night of emotional turmoil for me. Tom fully recovered, and I reached the point where I could believe that he was healthy and going to live for a long time. Even so, for years I made him promise that he would somehow make sure I died before he did. The grief still had that hold on me, and I just couldn't contemplate facing another loss. But through several experiences in the last few years, I have come to understand and accept that we don't get to place conditions on love – or on life. Friendship and love are gifts we give freely – they are not conditional on the recipient earning our gift or being worthy of it, and they are not conditional on a fairytale guarantee that we won't be hurt by giving the gift.

For almost twenty years, I found an excuse to <u>not</u> write what is in these pages. I told myself I was too busy, that no one would be interested, that I didn't know anything about writing books. But today, in writing these last few lines, I know that I was lying to myself. Those things might all be true – but they were not what made me choose not to write. I didn't write the story sooner because I was afraid the words would take me back to that dark place, and that I would again be lost there. And as I wrote, I did get drawn back, back to places of love and warmth and happy memories – reliving those feelings was an unexpected surprise that brought me great joy. But I also was drawn back to all the dark places. I could feel a change in me; I again felt the isolation and the pain, and could relive it as if they were here with me, in my life again. It was frightening to find that all those emotions are still there, still a part of me.

But what is most important is that I was <u>not</u> lost there.

I walked there and I am no longer afraid.

I am here. I am free. And the darkness will not hold me.

EPILOGUE

My life today is filled with so many blessings. My family has not once let me down – my mother and siblings with their spouses have been a source of strength, comfort, support, and inspiration – without exception. Tom – my husband of more than seven years! – and our eight children, their spouses/significant others, and our grandchildren are a constant source of wonder, joy, and contentment. I have three families of in-laws, all of whom are an important part of my life. My work is challenging, rewarding and full of surprises. Though I suffer through the same frustrations, disappointments and failures that tend to interrupt the lives of everyone, I always come back to the humbling realization of just how fortunate I am. So, I have tried to absorb a few lessons from my experiences, a few observations that might help me one day in the future.

The first lesson was one of practicality. It is so easy to believe that we will all reach old age; Bud and I had *never – never, discussed death.* I didn't even know if he had a preference between burial and cremation. The first few hours following the news of a spouse's death are not the time to be making important decisions – those things need to be discussed in advance. We each had life insurance policies payable to our children; what we had not even bothered to ask was at what age they would receive the funds. In Arizona, as well as in many other states, minors who are listed as beneficiaries of a life insurance policy receive the proceeds when they turn eighteen unless there is a Trust in effect. This was not good in our case: very few eighteen-year olds are wise in handling a sum of money that must seem larger to them than anything they have ever imagined.

A lesson of the heart that I learned was that, just as I'd had to understand there was no shame in needing help to cope, I also had to understand that depth of grief *is not measured by how much help is needed.* During the time I was lost after Bud's death, I knew someone who had remarried a few years after her husband's death, and at first I wondered how she could possibly have loved the deceased husband if she could remarry so soon. As my healing progressed, I finally understood that depression isn't a meter that reflects the severity of the loss. Grief and recovery are so individual, and the ability or lack of ability to cope is not a correlate to the depth of the loss.

My failure to share loss with others who were suffering *harmed more than just myself.* I now see the harm I did by shutting out my family; I saw it in their eyes after they read my story. It has only been through the writing of the story that I have been able to see how much I missed by not allowing myself to lean on my children; I am forced to wonder how different their lives might have been if I had been able to see and share their grief.

As I had awakened after each of my surgeries, I wished I could just go back to sleep until it didn't hurt anymore. The same is true for grieving, as well. Knowing intellectually that one day it will stop hurting doesn't help on the day that it still hurts so much. The lessening of the pain can be a very slow process, and sometimes I grew weary of hurting. And growing past the grief wasn't easy; it took a lot of work. Who would have thought it could be work to allow myself to have fun? I tried to reason with myself, and would ask, "If I could do anything fun that I wanted to do, what would it be?" The only answer I found at the time was that I couldn't think of anything that would be fun. I decided that such an answer was unacceptable; there had to be something in my life that would be fun. And of course there was – *it just wasn't easy for me to recognize or accept.* We sometimes have to make a conscious effort to seek out what might be available for us to enjoy.

Most importantly of all, I have learned that *resiliency resides in each of us.* If this wasn't true, we could not, even as a whole society, continue to survive the emotional devastation we suffer as we witness events around the world. Despair and hopelessness are probably not foreign to anyone; no single person has a corner on loss. I remember seeing the movie *Sea Biscuit* and telling my sister that my heart just could not hold all the emotion of the movie. Our hearts overflow often, and yet we can continue to dance in the sunshine and revel in the firelight; the color does return and the birds do sing again. If you have ever watched someone live a life of setback after setback, of difficulties brought on by self or by circumstances, you have seen that same flame of resiliency light the way.

I will always identify with those who grieve: I will always be able to feel again the cavernous empty spaces within my heart and I will never forget how it feels to nearly die of a broken heart. But I will always, always know that there can be recovery and healing ahead for that person who grieves, and my heart rejoices in the knowing of this, even as it aches in empathy for that person.

Today, I know that grieving can take place without being accompanied by clinical depression; as a research scientist, I have a far greater understanding of what happened within me to create the chasms. But while stuck in the bottom of a chasm, scientific elucidation provides nothing for you at all. The single most crucial factor in my two recoveries was making a connection. The first time, my connection was to a desire to not disappear forever, and the second was a connection to the instinct to do no harm. The body is a miraculous machine, and given the opportunity and proper conditions, it will heal; however, it often needs help to do so, and we must be willing to seek that help. The resiliency to heal is but one of the many gifts given to us by our Creator. Know that it is there. No matter what life holds, I plan to grab onto the healing and never let go. And I hope that you will always do the same.

AUTHOR'S NOTE

Though the focus of my professional research is vaccine development, I spend many hours researching health issues of particular interest to friends and family, which have included a broad range of topics: cancer, sleep apnea, stroke, Alzheimer's, frontal lobe dementia, addiction, heart attacks, and my own depression.

Another aspect of becoming a scientist is the profound appreciation I have gained for the complexities of our biology. Estimates of the total number of cells that comprise the human body are variable, but most fall into the category of mind-boggling. Some suggest the number is around a hundred trillion. I don't know about you, but I can't comprehend that number. The size of a human cell is about one-tenth the size of the smallest object our eyes are able to detect.

Yet within each of those tiny cells (many, many, many cells), multiple separate processes are taking place in every second of the day. Constant communication takes place, originating from a single cell or a group of cells which can then bring about substantial changes in other parts of the body. The efficiency for those communications varies from person to person. Our bodies, as technically advanced machines, are similar to the complex international systems of economics or finance, where a small ripple in one area of the world can release a cascade of events with massive repercussions in all other parts of the globe; so, too, can a ripple in one area of our bodies release a cascade of events with massive repercussions in other parts of our being.

Today we know that many biochemical and physiological aspects contribute to depression. Lack of appetite leads to an imbalance of chemicals in the bloodstream; the stresses resulting from depression cause special proteins to send out signals of distress that cause the brain to behave differently; genetics play a role by grouping genes in combinations that make one person more susceptible than another person to all kinds of health challenges, including clinical depression.

Knowing all these things today is reassuring to me in the sense that I can place a logical and unemotional ribbon around my depression and see that it is a bodily phenomenon that can be separated from the normal process of grieving. Very few of us will have a future that is never sad, never visited by the anguish of loss. Understanding that it is possible to mourn a loss, and yet avoid a chasm, is part of the support system that will keep me whole, as I am today.

ACKNOWLEDGEMENTS

*Finding the words to share a personal story is
a difficult challenge; no less difficult is finding
the words to thank those who made the telling
possible. The journey was never mine alone.*

My thanks go to my husband, Tom, who has been
with me through all the pages – even those that drew me
away from him to a distant place; who continues to celebrate the moments of our lives that touch his heart; who
bravely read each new revision with supportive anticipa-
tion and an eye for typos.

Our eight children – Gary, Ed, Kathy, Shane, Andie,
Michael, Angela, and Tony, and their spouses/significant
others – have each held a special role in the outcome of
the story, each has made the tapestry more vibrant and
warm. I am grateful to have the places in my heart that
each of them has claimed.

My mother and father, Marie and Bernie, gave me a
childhood rich in love, strength, and guidance. Each time
in my life that there has been a crisis to withstand or an
event to celebrate, they contributed in small and enormous ways to make that happen. My gratitude to them is
surrounded with joy and their song is with me always.

My siblings and their spouses: Fran and Larry, Ruth and Bob, Joyce and Marvin, Dennis and Julie – are all masters of generous giving. A warm embrace, a word of encouragement or advice, a gift of sustenance to the pantry or to the soul – I have watched them all my life give generously to strangers, to friends, to relatives. They have left footprints in the journeys of many; I am thankful to be among those who have received their love, laughter, teasing, wisdom and unwavering support.

My thanks to all the other members of my family, past and present, who have stood beside me in thought or with their presence, when we have gathered in joy or to say goodbye.

To my families of in-laws, thank you for welcoming me into your lives: Emmet and Margaret, Dawn, Tim, and Dixie; Geraldine, Jerry, Wyline, Mary, Joe, Jimmy, Colleen and Vicki; Clarence and Marge.

Pam, Diane, and Vicky – thank you for all the ways you tried to free me from the sadness: for sitting with me, for pushing me forward, for knowing when to be blunt and when to let me cry. Lee and Val – thank you for sharing my sorrow, for loving my children, and for bringing Tom into my life. My thanks to Patty, who became a friend to me and a second mother to Shane, who kept my loss from being even greater, and who is taller than I am in so many ways.

The road from writing the first word to printing the first book also requires the efforts of many; they were the ones who made the task less daunting and overcame the overwhelming.

My deep thanks and appreciation go to Karen Wittmer for reading my first draft and letting me know I should write a second or third draft; to Gloria Jacobs for her critical feedback, her suggested improvements and her kind inspiration; to Kathleen Todd, who walked me from the second chasm all those many years ago, and more recently walked me through needed additions to the story from a therapist's perspective; to Laura Orsini, the freelance editor who gave my words focus and clarity; to Dr. Aaron Krasnow, who read the manuscript with fresh objectivity to detect omissions. I am grateful to those who gave of their time to read the manuscript and share with future readers what they thought of it: Joyce Beck, Dr. Cláudia Bisol, Clifford Mark, Dr. Karen Peterson, Reverend Ronald Rehrer, and Marjorie Schulte.

Just how do you thank the person responsible for making the printed book available to those who would read it? Nancy Cleary, of Wyatt-MacKenzie Publishing, Inc., heard my voice and that of all those who are lost in depression and need help. And she answered. She is part of the circle, and I am so grateful to her for listening with her soul.

I have come to the acknowledgement that is the most difficult for me to express. During the fall of 1976, as my life was deteriorating and I thought I was crazy, a courageous woman was about to publish her story of clinical depression. *The Cracker Factory* was first published in 1977, which leads me to believe that at the same time as I was struggling to emerge from the first chasm, Joyce Rebeta-Burditt was struggling to find the words that would educate a society about the very real disease of depression. My life was changed by reading her words. The humbling experience of being able to thank her decades later was a moment as profound for me as the one described in the prologue to *The Second Chasm*. My gratitude to Ms. Rebeta-Burditt, for both those moments, is surpassed only by the generosity of the gifts she has given to all of us.

In memory of a life too short, I would also like to acknowledge Bud. Those who knew him still smile at the mention of his name; the day of mourning has ended, and healing has brought us peace.

RESOURCES

Kathleen Todd, the therapist who helped me leave the second chasm, has recommended the following resources for those whose lives are affected by clinical depression:

Healing Anxiety & Depression, by Daniel Amen and Lisa Routh.

The Cognitive Behavioral Workbook for Depression, by William Knaus and Albert Ellis.

The Mindful Way through Depression: Freeing Yourself from Chronic Unhappiness, by J. Mark Williams, John D. Teasdale, Jon Kabat-Zinn, and Zindel V. Segal.

You Can Heal Your Life, by Louise Hay.

ABOUT THE AUTHOR

 Karen Kibler was raised in a small farming community in Iowa. She earned her Bachelor's Degree from the University of Iowa in 1977, and soon after relocated to Arizona. She received a Ph.D. in 1997 from Arizona State University where she is now an Assistant Research Professor and the university Biosafety Manager. The focus of her current research is HIV vaccines and treatments. Prior to her career in science she held several positions in business, from receptionist to owner, though her resume also includes skills such as welding and heavy equipment operation.

Writing has been a long-time passion of hers; however, until the completion of *The Second Chasm*, her audience was restricted to family and college class professors.

www.TheSecondChasm.com

Printed in the United States
137598LV00001B/8/P